THE NEW COMPLETE NORWEGIAN ELKHOUND

Tyra av Kotofjell, Best in Show winner in Norway. Bred by Birger Gronvold (Norway), and owned by Olav Wallo, Runefjell Kennels (USA).

The New Complete

NORWEGIAN ELKHOUND

by

Olav Wallo

1970

HOWELL BOOK HOUSE INC.

845 THIRD AVENUE, NEW YORK, N.Y. 10022

Foreword

MY interest in, and admiration for, the Norwegian Elkhound goes back many years. To see dogs of this breed hunting in the field or forest, or posing in the show ring, has always been a thrill.

I like the simple, natural, true personality of this great hunting dog whose original characteristics and appearance remain unchanged. He has all the fine qualities that a breed could possibly inherit. The Elkhound today is rugged. He is one of the few breeds that could, if necessary, live off the land in the wilderness.

This book is dedicated to those who had the foresight and courage to retain the Elkhound in his natural state for us and future generations to enjoy. My hope is that he will be kept unchanged, and that wherever he goes, he will take with him the fresh fragrance of the forest.

Although the saga of the Elkhound is well known to the Scandinavian people, I hope that others will enjoy knowing more about the National Dog of Norway.

I wish to express my sincere appreciation to the Norsk Elghundklub for information obtained from *Om Elghunder og Elgjakt i Norge de Siste 50 Ar.* I am grateful for the cooperation of the many authorities who have contributed articles (these contributions are duly acknowledged in the text), and of the many fanciers who have so kindly submitted photographs of their dogs for use in the book.

OLAV O. WALLO

A royal moose hunt in Sweden. From left to right, Prince Wilhelm of Sweden, King Alphonso of Spain, and King Gustav of Sweden. The position of the badge on King Gustav's hat is important in that it indicates the success of the hunt.

An Elkhound's Humble Request

My saga in the United States goes back more than five decades, from a slow start with a few secluded breeders and owners who cherished my outstanding qualities to the rank I enjoy today— 35th in popularity of all breeds registered by the American Kennel Club. This is where I like to be, not too high up on the scale, and not too far down.

Above all else, I resent the stupid translation of my name that has unfortunately been imposed upon me from my beginnings in this land. They call me an ELKHOUND. I am not a hound. I don't look like a hound; I don't hunt like a hound; and I don't run like a hound.

I am smart, and for hunting, I am second to none. But I am a big game hunter, and my breed in the Scandinavian countries helps to harvest over 40,000 Elg every fall. (Note that I hunt Elg, not Elk. Elg translates in English to Moose.)

In the dog shows in Scandinavia, I am a member of Group I, the Northern Breeds (*Spisshunder*). This Group consists of Alaskan Malamutes, Siberian Huskies, Finnish Spitz, Greenlanders, Samoyeds, and many more. Although the countries of Northern Europe are not big and impressive, they have created in the *Spisshunder* a simple, true and healthy strain of dogs that make a beautiful sight in any show.

The late president Herbert Hoover with Ronnie av Glitre (929110). Ronnie, a son of immortal Skrub av Glitre ex Bringe II av Glitre, was presented to the President by the people of Norway as an expression of appreciation for what he had done for them in their World War I time of need.

They belong together. Perhaps someday the American Kennel Club will recognize the injustice that has been done through the years in not recognizing these breeds as a Group to themselves. The members of the strain are scattered, lost and strangers in the regular Groups.

For the judges, putting these dogs as a Group would certainly make strong sense, and make deciding among them more equitable. For the breeders and owners, it would be a grand homecoming—a family reunion. It is something for the leaders and protectors of purebred dogs in the United States to think about.

NOTE: In Norway, and most other European countries, the breed is known as the *Elghund*. In the author's opinion, this should be its name in America and England, too. However, to avoid confusion throughout most of the book we have referred to the breed by the American Kennel Club designation for it, the Norwegian Elkhound.

Mrs. Herbert Hoover and Ronnie av Glitre.

9

Boy av Glitre (d) , 8318
(Ch. Skrub av Glitre ex Gaupa II av Glitre)
Breeder-Owner: T. Hemsen
"av Glitre" Kennels, Norway

The Picture of Boy av Glitre

by Johnny Aarflot

(Mr. Aarflot, famous breeder, field trial and show judge, is one of the world's most respected authorities on the Norwegian Elkhound. This is a translated excerpt of an article by him in the Norsk Elghunds 50 Year Jubilee Book.)

I STILL consider this picture I took of Boy av Giltre (facing page) as the best illustration of a good Norwegian Elkhound.

The head is excellent—beautiful, and with the serious, alert expression so typical for an Elkhound. The fur forms a nice collar on the well-poised neck. Body and legs are harmoniously proportioned. (An Elkhound's legs will usually seem more frail in a photograph than they really are.) Notice the good straight forelegs, and the correct placement of upper arm and shoulder—important for the beautiful carriage of neck and front. Notice, too, the strong back with a beautiful top line, and the short, well-formed flanks. Boy's hind legs are correctly angulated at the knee and hock joints. Too extreme an angulation is atypical for the Elkhound. He is not a short distance sprinter. His typical gait is a somewhat short canter that he can keep up for hours, even in rugged country.

As the photograph clearly shows, Boy had good close paws. Particularly note the right hind paw. The tail is tightly curled, and is straight on the back. (The lighting in the photograph makes it appear that Boy had a fan tail, but this was not so.) The light harness marking (back of the shoulders) is very typical, as is the dark "saddle" formed by the dark tips of the covering hair on the sides of the chest, and across the front. The light coloring of the legs is also evident. One will often see Elkhounds with the dark color spread all the way down to the paws, and this is not very becoming.

But all of these are just details. What characterizes this picture of Boy above all else is his typiness, and the harmony of his build.

It is most important that we safeguard this original type, and not sacrifice any of it to eliminate less important details. A beautiful coat with good color, a first rate tail, nice dark eyes—all are commendable, but won't help much if the dog lacks the correct harmonious type of body, and the true characteristics of the Elkhound. For example, a short-legged, heavy and overbuilt Elkhound should not rate very high at a show, even if other features are first rate. Nor should a tall-legged, frail dog with a long back be given awards. We repeat—type is the important factor, details are secondary.

Contents

When the giant fell, emptiness prevailed over the wilderness.
(*photo by B. Kolby, Norway*).

1

The Saga of the Norwegian Elkhound

F ROM out of the hazy mists of prehistoric time came the man and the beast—walking not as friendly, devoted pals, but as deadly enemies. Neither asked quarter, nor gave it.

Again and again, the scene repeated itself: a wounded moose in flight, and following in its bloody trail the beast, and then the man, ready to fight over the prey.

Later, the man, king of the forest and the thinker, captured the young beast, fed it, and taught it to hunt, track, and trail. The two grew to work as a team, and when the beast located wild game, the man came and killed it.

Hunting was best in the spring of the year, when the snow melted in the day but froze at night. The snow crust would carry the man and the beast, but the heavy moose would sink through into the depth. The beast would growl and snarl in front of the moose, and fight to hold it back, so that the man could attack with his spear and his bow and arrows. That night, moose meat would cook over the fire. The beast could not bark in those days; his only expression of glee and sorrow was a wolf-like howl.

Many a snow has melted in the mountains since that time. Progress has rolled forward, the man has become civilized, and the beast is now the dog.

In Denmark's flat woods, where the *Veidefolket* (gypsy peoples) hunted and roamed, the *Torvmosehund* (swamp dog) was found. It is generally believed that he was the forerunner of our Northern breeds, including the Norwegian Elkhound. It is also assumed that the people migrated into Scandinavia from the South. Some came as free men, others as hunted. They roamed the wild country, hunted and trapped, and lived off what the valley gave, for the land was rich in wild game and fish.

Very little is known concerning the origin and the ancestry of the *Veidefolket*. But in their wanderings they left behind *modings* (rubbish dumps) that have provided a wealth of information for the modern archeologist. In these *modings,* not only in Denmark but also in Southern Sweden, tools and weapons have been found, and it has been established that both big and small game were hunted with *Torvmosehund.*

After the time of the *Veidefolket* came the Viking period, when the freeborn Norsemen sailed the open sea, and the dog was the steady companion of the hardy man. In battle on land or sea, the dog was an honored member of the crew. Should the commander be wounded in battle, he would be carried on board his Viking ship. His dog, dead of course, would accompany him as the burning ship set full sail on a straight course far out to sea to Odin's and Thor's kingdom, the Valhalla, home of all brave and courageous Vikings. No leader would be welcome to Valhalla if he came with scant earthly possessions. Odin is quoted as saying that they should come to Valhalla with the same amount of wealth as they had on the pyre.

In another period of the Viking regime, the king or commander would be buried with full accoutrements—with his ship, weapons, tools, and even his dogs; this was the case at Vistehulen, Jaeren, in the southwest part of Norway. There, Professor Brinchmann of the Bergen museum found relics of the stone age, including four skeletons of dogs, two of which were very similar in bone structure to modern Elkhounds. Expert archeologists presume that this grave dates back from 4000 to 5000 B.C.

Then there were such other finds as the dog skeletons in the famous Gökstad ship, and the clay bowl in the grave at Vallöby, which bore in bas-relief a hunting scene with Elkhounds.

Next, Christianity came to Norway and the glorious Viking period ended. With its passing, the Elkhound retrogressed. Christianity came not as peaceful, hymn-singing guidance, but as harsh, rough dominance. Many of Norway's great leaders left the country and settled in Iceland and Greenland. Many who could not leave and would not turn Christian were thrown into the dog den, there to be torn to pieces by vicious dogs, presumably large dogs imported from Southern Europe.

Some centuries later came the black death. Valley after valley was swept clean of people. The dead were not buried because there were no survivors left to dig the graves. Farmhouses rotted and fell to the ground. As nature took over, brush crept over fertile fields, turning them into a wilderness.

The year 1696 was a tragic one for the Finnish people, for the severe, killing frost early in August froze the lakes and rivers and ruined the crops. Hunger and famine were in store for these Suomis folks. Of the 450,000 Finns, an estimated 100,000 left their homes and began the arduous journey westward across fjords, through endless forests, and over mountains—a long wandering in the face of an onrushing winter. How many reached Norwegian soil is not known, but many a nameless grave was dug in the wilderness and forgotten.

In Norway, the Suomis people mainly settled in the deep forests, where they cut timber, built homes, grubbed the fields, and hunted. From the Norwegian government they received title to the land.

Between Oslo and Ringerike there was at that time the vast area of Krokskogen, a deep forest settled by the Finns, which was much like their native land. Even today in Krokskogen one finds many names of Finnish origin.

At that time Krokskogen was noted for its big game, such as moose and bear, and for large game birds, such as *tiur* and *orrhane*. It is a well-known fact those great hunters from Finland also used the Elkhound to hunt big birds. Even today, far removed as he is from this period, an Elkhound, seeing a big bird in a tree, will sometimes stand beneath and let bubble from his throat a sound that is like small silver bells ringing. The bird will be so fascinated that he will not notice the hunter, even at a short distance.

It was a common thing with my Elkhound, Fram, purchased from Eidsvold in 1918. A friend of mine, John Martinsen, shot two *tiur* in Sorumsmoen over Fram in 1919, and after that Martinsen and

Fram made many trips to Krokskogen and Hollaia. Martinsen stated that it was the most fascinating hunting that could be experienced, and he should know for he was one of the best moose hunters in Ringerike at that time. How many *tiurs* were shot over Fram could never be learned. But one thing is certain, Martinsen did not borrow Fram for company alone.

Some Elkhounds have inherited these unusual gifts, and will hunt birds as the breed has done from way back in time. Mr. and Mrs. Eugene Caza, of Lake Elmo, Minnesota, tell of this experience with their female, Dama av Dalysen: "When Dama was about nine months old, we took her pheasant hunting. She flushed some birds out of the bush for us, and one flew up into a tree. While we were getting a bead on the pheasant, Dama ran up to the tree and sounded out with a loud, clear voice that seemed to us like the ringing of bells. The pheasant was captivated by her call, enabling us to walk up close and shoot. From that time on, Dama has always greeted us with a beautiful call that sounds like ringing bells, and she also uses it to help us get our game whenever we go hunting."

In Norse history, the years from 1825 to 1845 are referred to as the Wolf Period. At that time, thousands of wolves swarmed into Norway from Finland and Northern Sweden. Long, lanky, bony, and hungry, they hunted in packs, killing everything in their way, including wild game, cattle, and people. Many outlying districts had to be abandoned, because the inhabitants dared not go outside for days and farm stock were killed right in the barns. In one valley, the wolves even killed 15 horses.

For the Norwegian Elkhound, the big-game hunter and also the guardian of home and livestock, these were trying times. Although he was a good fighter, the Elkhound always had to fight against great odds. Usually he wore an iron collar with sharp spikes pointing outward. In spite of this, many an Elkhound was torn to pieces by his deadly enemy.

In the south central part of Norway, the night of February 14, 1842, for many years was called Wolf Night (*Graabine*) for that was the occasion of the big fight between a pack of wolves and nine of the toughest Elkhounds in the Norderhove Valley. The dogs' leader was Fanarok the Fearless, the greatest fighter of them all. His little brother, Purven, was the runt of the litter and not much of a fighter or hunter. Fanarok was his brother's pal and guardian. And heaven help the poor creature that picked on Purven.

The night before the fight, Fanorok was locked securely in the barn to protect the cattle, while Purven, the housepet, somehow got outside. Fanarok, hearing the screams of the helpless Purven as he was being torn to pieces by the wolves, pounded on the heavy door trying to get out to help his unfortunate brother—but to no avail. The next morning Fanarok looked over the place where Purven was killed. Some frozen blood in the white snow, and a few fur pieces shivering in the wind were all that remained. Fanarok slowly smelled them, and then, when he found Purven's collar, he was sure of what had happened. He raised his great head and in the frosty morning sent a call to his breed, a call of sorrow and hatred, a challenge to his gang. From farm after farm came the answer. These Elkhounds were strong, seasoned hunters. They had tangled with the roughest moose, so the biggest bear could not scare them. They had felt the rush of air when the moose struck with his front hoofs only inches from their heads. They had leaped at the ferocious bear as he reared on his hind legs with his neck bent like a swan's.

As night approached and a full, bright moon rose over the frozen landscape, a lonely Elkhound in the middle of small Lake Juveren, where the snow was shallow and the footing good, howled his sorrow to the world and to the cold moon. Not far away, eight of his recruits waited in a swamp.

They did not have long to wait. A pack of wolves soon appeared on the lake, following their leader and fanning out in an attempt to encircle the Elkhound. The latter raced straight for the slough where his pals waited.

The wolves, in close pursuit, also headed for the slough. But there they were in for a big surprise. The attack came so fast and so furiously that they had no time to organize their defense. Open jaws with sharp fangs cut and ripped. With tremendous speed the Elkhounds swarmed over them and tore at the wolves' bodies. Some of the wolves were slammed down. Jaws strong as steel traps clamped shut on throats and did not reopen until the wolf, four legs helplessly fanning the air, dropped lifeless. Growls and screams could be heard for miles. More and more wolves appeared on the lake where they smelled blood.

Men came from farms and cabins. Armed with guns, axes, swords, and other weapons, they stood side by side in the deep snow at the shoreline. It was doomsday for the wolves! And many an account was settled! Most of the men were dealing out heavy blows in the middle of the fray, while others on the outskirts quickly dispatched the wounded wolves seeking to escape on crushed legs. The men, boiling over with many years of hatred and revenge, had no mercy.

The fight raged on for hours; then the wolves realized that they were trapped. They ran from one side of the lake to the other, but could find no path of escape. The men on the shoreline moved inward. The circle shrunk more and more. This was the end.

When the first beam of the February sun rose over the frozen landscape, 27 wolves were stretched out on the snow. For years after, the valley was free of the wolf plague. For the Norwegian Elkhound it was a grand day. As for the men of Norderhove, they proudly wore wolf coats from Norway's greatest wolf fight.

Rich in folklore is the saga of the Norwegian Elkhound. One of the most interesting legends is the story of Tore Ullin and his Elkhound, Bram. It all started at a mid-summer dance on Myrvold Mountain, where young and old came to dance, play, and drink for two days. From Kvernbro Valley came Kransen, a raw-boned fighter always handy with the knife, hated by most women and a friend of no man. Tore, from a neighboring valley, was a handsome, friendly young man, the strongest of them all. In a fight the second day, Tore killed Kransen and from that time on he was a hunted man.

Tore sped northward at night, alone except for Bram, who was with him. They came to a beautiful valley, where they lived in a hole in the mountain for many years. For food, they hunted both summer and winter. In the deep snow and the frost of the evening, Bram's tail became filled with ice and snow, and he dragged it after him like a broom. Then it happened that Tore, the hunted, took Bram's tail, curled it on the dog's back, and tied it with a leather thong. From that time on, according to the story, the Elkhound has had a curly tail.

After the Wolf Period, the woods of Norway were very quiet. No big or small game was left. Only in Osterdalen and Hedmarken did a small herd of moose remain; the rest had been killed by wolves. Among the few Elkhounds that remained, it was difficult to find good specimens. Only in a few secluded valleys did the better strains exist. Then man—breeder, hunter, friend—came to pick up the pieces, and give the breed new life.

Greta of the North, C.D., in a spectacular view taken at Sourdough Gap, Mt. Ranier. Owned by Jerry McClenaghan.

Home of Bamse Gram, owned by Consul Jens Gram,
Ask, Ringerike, Norway.

2

Norwegian Elkhounds
in Norway

THE year 1865 is memorable in Elkhound history as the year in which Bamse Gram, destined to be a trail blazer and model for the breed for years to come, was whelped. Later known as Gamle Bamse Gram, he was owned by Consul Jens Gram, of Ask, Ringerike, a well-known sportsman and hunter.

No pedigree goes back further than Bamse, and even though there was a good strain of bitches in Ringerike at that time, he must be given credit for the unusual quality of the stock in that district later. Bamse, who was one of the first free-running Elkhounds (*loshund*), is described as follows: body coarse and a trifle long, not long-legged, wide head, large erect ears, dark eyes, gray color with a mixture of dark to nearly white, and some brown on the legs.

The first bench show in Norway was held at the *Contraskjaeret*, in Oslo, on June 28–29, 1877, under the auspices of the Norsk Jeger og Fiskerforening, a Norwegian hunting and fishing club. There were present 124 hunting dogs, including fifteen "Bear and Elk Dogs." All the Northern breeds were shown in the same class. Peter Carlsrud's Grant took first prize and Thorvald Buttingsrud's Sikker was awarded second prize. Although Bamse Gram was present, he could not receive first prize because his owner was one of the judges. Arne Omsted, Jens Gram, and N. Anker officiated.

The second bench show was held on June 25–26, 1880, with 180 dogs, including twenty-eight Elkhounds. No first prize was given. A. Strande's Fin (a *loshund* with fifty moose to his credit) received second prize. In Norway it is customary even today to judge each dog on its individual merit rather than on a comparative basis. If one or more entries in a class so deserve, each of them may be awarded first prize. Should none be of good quality, no first prize is given, and the placings may be only second or third.

In June 1887 the third show took place in Oslo, but information as to placings is not available. The fourth all breed Norsk Kennel Klub Show, at Oslo, on July 25–26, 1898, had an entry of 260 dogs. Arne Omsted's Bamse, 107, won first prize in a class of twenty-three "Elk and Bear Dogs."

At the first specialty show of the Norsk Dyrehundklub, at Rena, Osterdalen, August 11–12, 1900, there were separate classes for *Graahunden* (Gray Elkhounds) and for *Finmarkshunden* (Black Elkhounds). Entries were thirty-seven dogs and five dogs, respectively. Judges were P. M. Anker, of Black Elkhound fame, Helge Fenn, I. F. Eckersberg, and Louis Saxlund. First prizes and honor prizes among the Grays went to Fin (H. Solberg), Kandix (J. C. Hals), and Kjaek (Walmsnes). Among the Blacks there were no first prizes.

In 1899 the Norsk Dyrehundklub was started by Louis Saxlund. Two years later a breed Standard for the Gray Elkhound was proposed; it materialized in 1906. Since then the Standard has been revised several times, the latest revision being in the spring of 1950. The name of the Norsk Dyrehundklub was changed in 1949 to Norsk Elghundklub.

In the early part of the twentieth century some of the outstanding Elkhounds were: Nero (J. Skagnaes); Pasop, 408 (Lars Suseg); Bring, 399; Max (T. Lier); Fin, 400 (T. Lier); Vaktmand, 1342 (O. H. Waagaard); and Skram, 1343.

At the first field trial for *loshunder* (free running) Elkhounds in 1915, there was only one entry. At the next one, two years later, three were present. Then there were no more trials until 1948, after which the fixture has been an annual event, thanks to the efforts of the Elghundklub officers, Reidar Strömme, Erik V. Enberg, Sven Mjearum, and Dr. J. Hallingby.

The first Norwegian Elkhound bench show champion was Sara, 2118 (Fin ex Signe), whelped in 1912, bred and owned by Ole

Gamle Bamse Gram, owned by Consul Jens Gram, Ask, Norway.

Blegeberg, Nedre Eggedal. She finished in 1916 and was later sold and exported to Sweden.

Several of the early American imports were by Smik ex Lova, bred by Hans Fosse, of Lifjell Kennels.

One of the most noted Elkhounds of all time was Senny II, 2119 (Fram, 1518, ex Senny, 1087), whelped June 20, 1911, bred by Gullik Rua, Jondalen. He sold her to veterinarian T. Hemsen as foundation stock for his famous "av Glitre" Kennels. Rua kept the strain intact with Senny III, IV, V, VI, and VII. Senny V was exported to America and Senny VI became a Norwegian champion.

A STUDY IN LINE BREEDING

Pedigree of **CH. SKRUB** av **GLITRE**
Whelped January 25, 1923
Bred and Owned by T. Hemsen, Ski, Norway

```
                              Drey  (H. Fosse)
                    Grim  (NKKS-2867)
                              Maud  (S. Sjolie)
              Jack  (NKKS-2570)
                              Finn  (N. Hansen)
                    Froya  (S. Hetland)
                              Binna I  (NKKS-1526)
      Dyre av Glitre  (NKKS-4994)
                              Fram  (NKKS-2085)
                  * Fram  (NKKS-1518)
                              Bella  (NKKS-2578)
              ° Senny II  (NKKS-2119)
                              Bring  (NKKS-399)
                  + Senny  (NKKS-1087)
                              bitch owned by H. Gron


  CH. SKRUB av GLITRE  (d)  NKKS-6687


                              Fram  (NKKS-624)
                    Bob  (NKKS-2076)
                              Let III  (Wangaard)
              Bjonn  (NKKS-3189)
                              * Fram  (NKKS-1518)
                  ° Senny II  (NKKS-2119)
                              + Senny  (NKKS-1087)
      Gaupa av Glitre  (NKKS-5450)
                              Engrav's Storm
                    Finn  (NKKS-2860)
                              Nora  (NKKS-940)
              Jerva av Glitre  (NKKS-4191)
                              * Fram  (NKKS-1518)
                  ° Senny II  (NKKS-2119)
                              + Senny  (NKKS-1087)
```

26

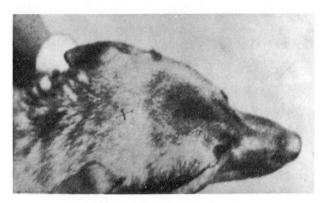

Ideal Elkhound Skull (Ch. Skrub av Glitre).

Skrub av Glitre.

Rua was careful not to inbreed. In contrast, Hemsen line-bred closely to Senny II for a number of generations and then outcrossed to Jack, 2570, for a fresh bloodline. The breeding programs of both men have produced champions. Skrub av Glitre on the one hand and Senny VI on the other. But of the two, the line breeding to Skrub seems to have yielded better results. Skrub was considered the handsomest Elkhound ever shown, while as a producing sire, he rated along with Gamle Bamse Gram. It is pointed out that Skrub carried 50% of the blood of Senny II.

T. Hemsen, who is an honorary member of the Norsk Elghund-klub, finished three champions, all in 1928: Ch. Skrub av Glitre (dog), 6687; Ch. Peik II av Glitre (dog), 6681; and Ch. Bringe II av Glitre (bitch), 6696. Starting with Senny II, Hemsen won consistently with his dogs up to 1949. More than a dozen of his well-known strain have come to America in the last thirty years.

Hans Christiansen (Gjetemyra Kennels), Oslo, raised three champions, all with Ch. Skrub av Glitre in their pedigrees: Ch. Binna av Gjetemyra (bitch), 8345; Ch. Laila av Gjetemyra (bitch), 8351; and Ch. Roy av Gjetemyra (dog), 10763. When this breeder died in 1938, his kennel was disbanded.

Ch. Binna av Gjetemyra went to the Skromtefjell Kennels of Sven Mjearum, Oslo, long-time secretary of the Norsk Elghundklub, who bred her to Boy av Glitre, 8318, a son of Ch. Skrub av Glitre. Later he mated her to her grandson, Falk av Skromtefjell, 76A. Through the many generations in the Skromtefjell line, one will find, even today, a high percentage of Ch. Skrub av Glitre and Senny II.

One of the oldest and best known kennels in Norway is Elglia, owned by J. Aarflot, a popular international judge of Elkhounds. He has judged the breed three times in America, where his opinions are earnestly sought. Undoubtedly his most famous dog was Ch. Saga of Elglia, 8800 (Ch. Skrub av Glitre ex Mausi), whelped on St. Patrick's Day 1929. She had litters by Ch. Skrub av Glitre and by Bjonn. In 1936, she was imported to America by Thomas White, where she had six champions to her credit.

Olav Campbell (av Tallo Kennels) raised Ch. Trysil-Knut av Tallo, 467L, and many other good hunting dogs. He, too, bred to Ch. Skrub av Glitre with his Binna back in 1931. Later, he had litters from Geira av Tallo by Ch. Steig av Jarlsberg and by Grei.

Mention should be made of Erik V. Enberg (Elgstolen Kennels)

Senny II, bred by Gullik Rua, Norway, and owned by
T. Hemsen.

T. Hemsen, Norway, with Senny II and her offspring.

29

in Oslo. Best known were his Elgstolens Buster, the sire of many good ones and a proven hunter with many moose to his credit, and Elgstolens Jerv, the famous hunter and field trial winner. Their pedigrees were strong in Gjetemyra blood.

Victor Jensen (Homanskogen Kennels) also had Gjetemyra stock, for he started with Ch. Laila av Gjetemyra, 8351. C. F. Langes (av Honn Kennels) specialized in hunting dogs. Charles Stavseth (Stavsetra Kennels) sent several fine dogs to America, including Ch. Stravsetras Lars, by Fyr, 62A. Nor can one forget Ivar Bo (Kirkemo Kennels) with his Ch. Grei av Kirkemo, 460C, and Harold Sommerstad (Glennas Kennels) wit Ch. Glennas Dolly, 1782K, Ch. Glennas Skrub, 1781K, and Ch. Jerva, 3448H.

Also prominent in the 1950's were the dogs of Consul E. A. Cappelen Smith (Fjeldheim Kennels), Reidar Stromme (Sorvangen Kennels), Toralf Raanaas (Ryfjeld Kennels) and Sten Abel (Listua Kennels). Others active in the breed included Carl Opseth, T. Amundsen, Thorstein Brenneng, Carl Michaelson, A. R. Arneson, P. Larson, S. J. Naess, and Jacob P. Holseng.

Then there is Gerd Berbom, who came to Norway after living in England for a number of years, and brought with her the lovely bitch, Ch. Anna of the Hollow, 1390D. Her Jarlsberg Kennels have produced many outstanding dogs.

One thing that has contributed greatly to the advancement of the Norwegian Elkhound has been the planned breeding program. Periodically, stud dogs have been selected by a supervisory committee of the Norsk Elghundklub.

Gerd Berbom's Jarlsberg Kennels holds the rare honor of having had three of its stud dogs on the club list at the same time—Ch. Steig av Jarlsberg, Eng. & Nor. Ch. Bamse av Jarlsberg, and Brisk av Jarlsberg.

Ch. Steig av Jarlsberg, 891G, was the standout. He was a masculine dog of exceptional quality, well-known as a hunting dog, and the sire of ten champions—seven in Norway, and three in America. His Norwegian champions included the bitches Moa, Bonnie and Silva av Jarlsberg, and the dogs Lorik, Buster, Holse, and Storm. (Buster, 1489Z, won the first Best in Show in Norway at the Annual International Show in Oslo on May 30–31, 1953, defeating 891 dogs of all breeds including 68 Elkhounds.) Steig's American champions were Am. & Can. Ch. Paal av Jarlsberg, Pelle av Jarlsberg, and

Elgstolens Buster and Elgstolens Jerv. Owned by Erik V. Enberg, Oslo.

Precilla av Jarlsberg. His progeny that have scored in the Winners class in Norway include: Strix av Jarlsberg, Andor, Rapp, Grim, Raggen, Nora and Rolly. Many of the present stud dogs on the NEK list carry his blood in their pedigree.

Ch. Tortaasen Ola, bred by
Jakob P. Holseng Norway,
and owned by Olav Wallo.

Ch. Grei av Kirkemo, bred
by Alf Opsahl, Norway,
and owned by Ivar Bo.

Vaktmand, owned by O.
H. Waagaard, Norway.

Ch. Saga av Elglia, by Ch. Skrub av Glitre ex Mausi, owned by Thomas H. White.

Ch. Steig av Jarlsberg, bred by Gerd Berbom, and owned by Hildur Almo.

Ch. Jerva, bred by A. Hoff (Norway) and owned by H. H. Sommerstad, of Oslo.

Excellent hunting type. Jerv av Elglia, winner at Oslo,
1936. Owner, Olav Campbell.

Ulvungen av Elglia (in 1946), bred by J. Aarfloot.

NORWEGIAN ELKHOUNDS IN NORWAY (1958–1968)
(Compiled with the assistance of Gerd Berbom)

Over the last decade there has been but small variation in the number of Elkhounds registered in Norway each year. In 1962, there were 790 new registrations; 1963, 778; 1964, 819; 1965, 754; and in 1966, 719. However, Norwegian Kennel Club statistics show that the Elkhound has dropped to fourth place in breed registrations. The Miniature Poodle is on top, and the English Setter has taken over the Elkhound's spot in second place. Oddly enough, this is despite a growing interest in the breed, with larger number of Elkhound breeders and exhibitors than ever before, and larger entries at the Elktrial. The explanation is that the other breeds have grown at an even greater pace.

The 1960 show of the Norsk Elghund Klub was the largest in its 60-year history, with an entry of 156 individual gray and 8 black Elkhounds. The following won in Winners class: *Dogs*—Trym, 57/2360; Trygg, 59/2504; Tuftetuns Kark, 58/3652; and Boss, 58/5240. *Bitches*—Binna, 58/2991; Illja, 57/2360; Tuftetuns Siki, 58/236; and Ruska, 57/3317. Trym and Illja are owned by Audun Sylten. Tuftetuns Kark and Tuftetuns Siki were bred by Ingvar Granhus. Siki is the dam of several good ones, bred by her new owner, Georg Kalager.

Well-known kennels currently producing dogs and bitches of high standards in Norway include: *Grafjell,* owned by Jon Rua; *Elgens,* Kristian Svestad; *Ryfjelds,* T. Raanaas; *Kalagerasens,* Peder Kalager; *Klegglias,* Kr. Bleka; *Kotofjell,* Birger Gronvold; *Suteras,* Christian and Oscar Svae; *Tuftetuns,* Ingvar Granhus; *Oftenasen,* Magne Aftrat; *Valpasen,* Aagot and Elizabeth Harbitz; *Tortasens,* Jacob P. Holseng; and *Sokomdal,* Arne Furuseth.

Among present day stud dogs, top rating must go to Klegglias Storm, 61/7943. Storm, bred by Kristian Bleka, is owned by Birger Gronvold, of Kotofjell prefix. One litter by Storm ex Lotte av Kotofjell included Varg, Fell, Lussy, and the now very famous Driv av Kotofjell—all dogs of exceptional quality.

Lussy was bought by Jens Semb Nygaard, and gained two Certificates. At her new home, she had but one litter of puppies (by Bjorn, 60/4940) before she tragically died while hunting at only two years of age. Puppies from this litter were exported to America and Canada.

The foremost Norwegian Elkhound of the day on the continent—Ch. Driv av Kotfjell.

Driv av Kotofjell, owned by Reidar Stromme, has enjoyed fantastic success in the show rings of Scandanavia. He has been honored as "the foremost winning dog of the year," and was the first dog to win the "Bamse" trophy, newly instituted by the Norsk Kennel Club, and completed for at 6 NKK shows each year. The trophy is named for the first dog to be registered by the Norsk Kennel Club in 1898. Naturally "Bamse" was an Elkhound, the proud native breed.

Another son of Klegglias Storm that is impressing is Bjorn av Kotofjell, 62/2666. His dam is Tussi, 58/4822.

The Tortasens Kennels, owned by Jacob P. Holseng, is another that is enjoying good fortune in selective breeding. From this kennel came world famous Nor. and Am. Ch. Tortasens Bjonn II, a distinguished winner and a stud dog of considerable merit even before his exportation to the United States. Of equal pride for Tortasen was Ch. Moa, 1491-Z, the first Elkhound bitch to win a Group at an NKK show. Moa was dam of Bjonn II and his fine litter brother, Tortasens Garm, 53/509, and of the two outstanding bitches—Tortasens Sussi, 53/648 (sired by Ch. Bamse) and Tortasens Kaisa, 55/509 (sired by Buster). Kaisa is owned by Ingvar Granhus.

Jon Rua (Grafjel Kennel), well-known beeder and exhibitor, carries on the famous bitch name of "Senny."

The Valpasens Kennels of the Misses Aagot and Elizabeth Harbitz are breeders of Rugg av Valpasen, 56/2694 (by Ch. Ruggen 39120 ex Bamsi, 54/2694), who has won a 1st Winner and Certificate. Lately the Misses Harbitz have given some of their interest to another Spitz breed, the Norsk Lundehund (Puffin dog). This breed, used for hunting the Puffin bird on the isle of Vaeroy in north Norway, is still very limited in number, and unknown outside of Norway.

Ivar Nordby has a top bitch in Tuftetuns Morsa, 59/1288 (by Boss av Glisefyr, 56/913 ex Tortasens Kaisa, 55/509). She is the dam of Tuftetuns Binna, 60/2579. Jacob Simonsen, field trial enthusiast, owns the fine bitch Binna, 65/3443 (by Bertil, 62/1810 ex Blondi, 63/2008).

A relatively new breeder is Ivar Arntzen, who has exhibited four young ones out of the same litter with exciting success.

Ch. Tass, 62/4360, select stud dog, owned by Signe Furuseth.

The present day stud dog list contains the following names:
Nor. & Sv. Ch. Tass, 62/4360 (Owner, Signe Furuseth)
Ch. Grei, 61/4473 (Owner, Ole Saebo)
Ch. Heiki, 59/2755 (Owner, Einar Foll)
Ch. Varg, 60/5802 (Owner, Kr. og Jacog Hellenes)
Ch Star, 62/3209 (Owner, Odd Venas)

Some other noteworthy dogs on the current scene are Trym, 57/2360 (by Bamse, 30840 ex Topsy av Suteras, 5686S), owned by Audun Sylten, and Bamse, 59/2137 (by Ch. Storm ex Bamsi 57/3620), bred by Salve Haland and owned by Anders Blomhaug. Ch. Kalagerasens Bamse, 61/4731, closely line-bred to Ch. Steig av Jarlsberg, is a Certificate Winner with a 1st at a Field Trial. Bred by Peder Kalager, he is owned by Halvard Christiansen.

Bertil, 62/1810 (by Lovtangens Rollo, 1720 ex Senny, 58/335), owned by Kjell Dokken, has been used a lot for breeding because of his hunting abilities.

A successful sire is Burmann, owned by the brothers Oscar and Christian Svae. Birger Gronvold has also used Burmann effectively with the bitches Trine, Nurri, and Lotte av Kotofjell. Burman, 59/1992 (by Ch. Storm, 54/1359 ex Ch. Tussi av Suteras, 6410), bred by Christian Svae, has also been used for a lot of breeding with good result.

A few words concerning the shows in Norway might be of interest. Show dogs are not clipped or trimmed. Even the whiskers are not cut. The nails are expected to be worn down from work afield. A top Elkhound should be able to hunt in the forenoon and be shown in good form in the afternoon. It is a good plan to give the dog a bath prior to the show, if necessary. He should be in good weight so as to present the desired square appearance with wide and deep loin.

Once a year the breed judges meet to examine ten Elkhounds chosen at random, and to discuss their conformation in writing, with the purpose of obtaining a composite picture of the ideal Elkhound.

To qualify as a champion dog or bitch in Norway, an Elkhound must win three Firsts in Winners class with Certificate, under at least two different judges, and must also score a 1st, 2nd, or 3rd prize at a Field Trial. This last requirement was introduced some years ago, and is to a great extent the reason for the relatively small number of champions qualified in recent years. The official NKK list gives the following names:

Ch. Tass, 62/4360, owned by Signe Furuseth
Ch. Fjall, 60/3543, owned by A. Christiansen, Sweden
Ch. Storm, 54/1359, owned by Ole Aalerud
Ch. Blix, 53/2468, owned by Birger Berggard
Ch. Tortasens Garm, 53/509, owned by Gjermund Lynnebakke
Ch. Tortasens Bjonn II, 53/643, previously owned by Jesper Hallingby
Ch. Driv av Kotofjell, previously owned by Reidar Stromme, but sold to Werner Andersson in Sweden in 1968.

Among current Winners are: Ajaks, 64/732, (by Bjornemoens Bamse, 60/1109 ex Bessie 61/1892) ; Tass, 62/4360, (by Boss, 58/4240 ex Trine av Suteras, 58/108) ; Peik, 63/736 (by Buster, 61/4541 ex Tonnie, 59/4932) ; and Tatnoss, 62/7540 (by Boss av Flisefyr) .

Jens Semb Nygaard's dog Bjorn, 60/4940 (by Bjorn 56/1331 ex Topsy) , a homebred, has six Certificates to his credit in Norway and Sweden. The most remarkable was at the NKK Oslo show in 1964, where he scored 1 VK, Cert. CACIB, AEP, BOB, Best in Group, and Best in Show.

Bjorn is the sire of a yet-young dog, Star 67/3367. The dam is Lussy of Kotofjell. Star won his junior classes and beat the Winner class dog to go Best of Breed, and place Reserve in the Group at the NKK 1967 show.

Another winner of today is Solvbamse (Silverbamse), 61/4781 (by Storm av Suteras ex Nyste), owned by Trygve Kopstad. Solvbamse is a Group winner, and has a Field Trial first.

Over recent years, quite a number of Elkhounds have been exported to America, and lately, also to France. One of the more significant of the last was the exportation by Arne Furuseth of his lovely homebred bitch, Dolly av Sokomdal, 66/6831 (by Nor. & Sv. Ch. Tass ex Konny). Sent to Mme. D. Cousin, Dolly was entered at Evian show, and got CAC. Mme. Cousin has become a strong enthusiast of the breed.

Some time ago, a very interesting discovery was made at Hov Farm, north of Oslo. In a water-logged country, at a depth of 17.5 meters, an elk-revier (horn) was found. It is probably the oldest to be discovered thus far, being dated by radiologic science to be about 8,000 years old. (There may be a difference of 160 years, either way, in establishing the correct age.) The horn is in good condition, which is believed to be due to the fact that it had been dropped by the elk in a bog.

Ch. Klegglia's Storm, owned by Birger Gronvold, Kotofjell Kennels, Norway.

3

The Black Elkhound of Norway

LITTLE is known outside of Norway about the Black Elk and Bear Dog with its interesting history, which parallels in many ways that of the Gray Elkhound. As a breed, it is fast disappearing from Scandinavian shows and kennels. Although efforts have been made from time to time to revive the popularity of the black variety, most of the breeders have become discouraged and the results have not been satisfactory.

In his *Field Sports of the North of Europe* (1827–1828), Captain Llewellyn Lloyd, the famous British big-game hunter, was among the first to describe the Black Elkhound. He purchased two dogs in Norway, both of which were described as coal black. One of them, called Hector, he acquired from Daniel Anderson, Aasnes, at a good price. Since Anderson was a great bear hunter, Hector had many bears to his credit. The other Black Elkhound, Paijas, was said to be very handsome and courageous.

From 1880 to 1890, the breed was fairly common, especially in Osterdalen and Hedemarken. But from then on, the Gray Elkhound took the lead.

P. M. Anker, Fredrikshald, was one of the first to produce outstanding dogs of the black breed. At the 1898 dog show in Oslo, where both gray and black dogs were exhibited in the same class, his Bjorn was awarded first prize. In 1900, with classes separated by

Black Elkhound, Fin. Owned by
Paulus Lunde, Larvik, Norway.

color, Bjorn again received first prize. And the following year in
Drammen, he won the Norsk Kennel Klub Honor Prize. Anker's
most noted dog, Ola, was a well-known hunter, reputed to be smart
in approaching moose and to be a terrific fighter.

F. M. Treschow, who bred black dogs for a number of years,
finally discontinued his breeding activities because his breeding
stock did not possess the necessary hunting ability.

Others who should be mentioned in connection with the breed
include: Ingv Svelle, Asbjorn Hustad, L. O, Kjellemo, and Paulus
Lunde. In later years there were Ole Kjornes, Dr. Grythe, Johs.
Mustrop, and O. Kvernberg.

The Black Elkhound is medium-sized and built a little lighter
than the gray dog. He must be jet black, not brownish black, and
with no large off-color markings.

Sven Mjearum and Erik Enberg, breeders of Gray Elkhounds,
have turned their attention to Black Elkhounds. That this grand
old breed is making some progress in a return to its former popularity is gratifying, for the Black Elkhound should not be permitted
to become extinct.

4

The Norsk Elghund Klub Honorary Members

(Translated from Birger Bergrav's tribute to Omsted and Platou in Om Elghunder og Elgakt i Norge de Siste 50 Ar).

SECRETARY Carl Omsted, from his birth on May 3, 1867, to his death on August 23, 1941, was warmly interested in cynology and especially in the Norwegian Elkhound. In fact, if it had not been for Carl Omsted's energetic efforts in behalf of the breed, there would have been no Gray Elkhounds today. Thus he might well be called the creator of the modern Elkhound. Many years of hard work, much patience, knowledge, and experience were required. All these things Carl Omsted possessed in full measure. I believe that he was a judge even prior to the formation of the Norsk Kennel Klub and the Norsk Dyrehundklub. His "eye" for correct type, combined with his knowledge and experience in hunting qualified him for the task of selecting the foundation stock from various parts of the country. It was necessary to encourage the breeders and to instill in them more life and interest in their work. The weeds had to be pulled with a strong hand and that hand was Carl Omsted's. Whenever a question had to be settled or advice was needed, Omsted was ready and helpful in all hours of day or night. He had the satisfaction of seeing his work produce a rich and wonderful harvest. Then he was glad. His eyes would sparkle when he brought out a good, typical specimen. When Ch. Skrub av Glitre made his triumphant march, Carl Omsted was with him. The Norsk Dyrehundklub and the Norsk Kennel Klub made him an honorary member in 1935.

As a judge, he officiated for many years, and it was always a gala occasion when he was in the show ring. He was strict, but fair and square. Now that the Elkhound is recognized and registered in all countries due to his splendid efforts, let us hope that his life and the task he completed for our benefit will live and be an inspiration for us and the coming generation.

H AROLD PLATOU was in his own right an honorary member of the Norsk Dyrehundklub. He carried on where Carl Omsted left off. And even before that, he worked hard to bring the Elkhound breed up to standard.

He was an outdoorsman to the very tips of his fingers, although he was reared in the city. He was born October 29, 1877, in Oslo, and died September 23, 1946. He started hunting as a fifteen year old and enjoyed over half a century of sport in the woods and mountains. Ornithology was his special interest.

For many years he was secretary of Norges Jaeger og Fisker Forbund, a foreman of the Norsk Dyrehundklub, and a director of the Norsk Kennel Klub. There are few who have not benefited by his good advice. Friendly as he was, he had the uncanny ability to solve problems of others. Furthermore, he was gifted with a professional manner, high culture, and a winning personality. As a judge in field trials and bench shows, he was always highly regarded. Seldom was there a show in which he did not judge the Northern breeds, but he devoted most of his time to Elkhounds, which he tried to bring into the limelight.

It was fun in the ring when he judged and it was fun with him at the trials. All were very pleased with him, looking up to this man possessed with physical and mental fortitude and a friendly handshake.

44

Many words of appreciation were spoken at his funeral. And we were with him in spirit when these words were sung:

"There flies a bird o'er forest heights
He sings the well-known songs.
He calls me off the beaten way
Along the shady trail.
I reach the hidden spring and pool,
Where moose their thirst allay,
And still the bird song's far away
With the hum and sigh of winds.
Tirili Tove, Tirili Tove
Far, far away in the distant woods."

Trygg av Skromtefjell, bred by Sven Mjearum, Norway, and owned by Ole Omlid.

5

Norsk Kennel Klub
Honorary Award

By the fire outside the cave sat a stone age man, fingering some sharp flints and a small piece of oak, weather-dried by wind and storm. On the other side of the fire, a dog slept, tired after the day's hunt and full-fed on the day's prey—sleeping with his body, but not with his senses. His pricked ears, always on guard, searched for the smallest sound. His nostrils vibrated and sucked in all the smells, even in his sleep.

Suddenly, all alive, the dog stood up on straight legs with withers bristling and all muscles tense. From down in his throat gurgled forth warning of the threat of a wolf pack far in the wilderness. The dog knew that a wolf never ventured close to smoke from a fire, but it is a dog's task to announce the presence of quarry or enemy. It is the hunter's job to kill.

With his simple tools, primitive understanding and overall vision, the man carved the image of the dog as he saw it. He had no gift for details and no use for them, but he knew the dog from the long day and night hunting that had made them a team.

The carving was created by artist Arne Tjomsland as an award to be given by the Norsk Kennel Klub to persons who have in a deserving way promoted good-will toward the club and dogdom. H. M. King Olav, of Norway, was the first person to receive this wonderful trophy.

Ch. Gra-Val's Rolf, first Norwegian Elkhound to win Best in Show in the United States. Bred by Grace E. Vail. Owned by David N. Klegman, Tarzana, Calif.

6

The Norwegian Elkhound in America

JUST when the Elkhound first came to America is not definitely known, but the earliest record of the breed in this country apparently is the registration of three Elkhounds in the 1913 American Kennel Club Stud Book:

Koik 170389 (Rap II ex Bibbi) whelped March 1909, gray
Bimba 170390 (Bamse ex Bibi) whelped June 1910, gray
Laila, 170391 (Hay ex Binna) whelped July 1910, gray

These three imports (bred by O. Hykket, Carl Olmstead, and B. Larsen respectively, all of Oslo, Norway), were owned by Gottlieb Lechner, Weiser, Idaho. The offspring of these dogs were widely distributed.

Some of them went to R. D. Williams, Lexington, Kentucky, who mated them with his own dogs. In his Rookwood Kennels were Norseman, Trondhjem, Svelikin, and others. His stock was acquired by Walter Channing and Bayard Boyesen, both pioneers in Elkhound breeding in America.

About 1914, Mrs. William Farquhar, Hempstead, Long Island, raised a litter sired by Mich Mich. Registrations were few indeed; in fact, only twenty-two Elkhounds were registered in the decade following 1912.

The Norwegian Bear Dog, Lady Hilda, won first in the Open Class at Los Angeles in 1913. And the Norwegian Elkhound, Mich

Mich, won first in the Open Class at Mineola in 1914. Three years later, Gretchen won at the same show.

It was not until 1924 that the American public obtained its first impression of the breed at Westminster, when imported Ch. Crimm of Lifjell, 385780 (Smik ex Lova) was placed fourth in the Miscellaneous Class. At the next two Westminster shows, at which the Elkhound was exhibited in its own breed classification, Grimm was Best of Breed. This dog and his litter sister, Baldra of Lifjell, 385779, had been imported in 1923 by Walter Channing (Brixton Kennels), Dover, Massachusetts. Shortly afterward, Baldra had a fine litter sired by Bamse.

In 1924 the imports started to arrive. Bayard Boyesen (Vindsval Kennels) Winchester, New Hampshire, imported five Elkhounds from Norway:

> Ch. Heika av Glitre (dog) 427257
>   (Dyre av Glitre ex Gaupa av Glitre)
> Heia (bitch) 438887 (Fink ex Bella II)
> Bringe av Glitre (bitch) 438477 (Jack ex Senny II)
> Lydi (Bitch) 430888 (Gubben ex Heia)
> Rugg (dog) 438476 (Smik ex Lova)

Heika, carrying 50% of the blood of that famous Norwegian bitch, Senny II, sired five champions, among which were Ch. Vaaben av Vindsval, 840759, and Ch. Vakker av Vindsval, 876081. Best of Breed at Westminster four years in succession, Heika was of ideal type, powerful and compact, with wedge-shaped head, straight, short back, and perfect tail carriage. Heika, a massive bitch of tremendous bone and substance, was credited with six bears in one winter. Linebred to Skagnae's Bamse, she whelped eight puppies by Fin soon after her arrival in this country. Bringe, a daughter of Senny II, was winner of the "Prize of Honor" for 1921. Rugg, a son of that grand old hunter Smik, was famous in the show ring as well as in big-game hunting in Norway. Baruse, 44514, a brother of Rugg, was imported in 1925 by Walter W. Bagge, Des Plaines, Illinois. Then there was Finna, 467389, in whelp to Tas, brought over by Dr. Leon F. Whitney, famous author of many books on dog breeding and care.

On the West Coast, William H. and Cedelia Maxwell, Lakeside, Washington, who imported Senny V, 646103, from Norway, raised and sold many Elkhounds.

Ch. Helka av Glitre, bred
by C. T. Johnsrud, Norway,
and owned by B. Boyesen.

Rugg, bred by Hans Fosse
(Norway), and owned by
Vindsval Kennels, Mass.

Heia, bred by P. Jenshagen
(Norway), and owned by B. Boyesen.

The first import from England on record was Bon Bjerke, 649806, who came across the Atlantic in 1928. The following year W. F. Holmes of England sent over the first of many Elkhounds bearing the "of the Holm" suffix, Oscar of the Holm, 700962, by Finnegutten. These imports greatly improved the native breeding stock. In addition to the breeders already mentioned, there were J. W. Essex, Seattle, Washington; Mrs. Lucas Combs, Lexington, Kentucky; John B. Brainerd, Enfield, Massachusetts; and Winsor Gale, Weston, Massachusetts.

The first import from Scotland was Ch. Vingo of Inverailort, 742889, bred by Mrs. C. H. J. Cameron-Head. He sired more than a score of fine Elkhounds, including five Kettle Cove champions, three of which were from imported Goro of the Fjiords. Vingo, by Finnegutten, was the first Elkhound to win Best of Breed at both Morris and Essex (in 1933) and Westminster (in 1932). The good-headed, imported Ch. Binne av Glitre 747169, repeated the feat and so did imported Ch. Bjonn, 852513. Bjonn, who sired two Lindvangen champions in 1935, had a well-proportioned body and excellent tail but is reported to have had a rather narrow skull.

From Canada came Bringe av Solskin, A-261159, and from Sweden came Rapp av Gra, A-280725, owned by George H. Earle III, then Governor of Pennsylvania. It is said of Rapp, who was Best of Winners at Westminster in 1938, that he had good substance but that his tail was not tightly curled.

Elkhounds were associated with other famous people. For instance, imported Ronnie av Glitre, 929110 (Skrub av Glitre ex Bringe II av Glitre), bred by T. Hemsen, Norway, was owned by President Herbert Hoover. An Elkhound from the Glitre Kennels was a gift to the President from the people of Norway, a small but precious token for what he did for his friends over there in their hour of need after World War I. The President transferred one of his Elkhounds, Belleau of Elglia, to Commander C. E. Rosendahl, of Akron, which was with the fleet in the Pacific. Another Elkhound fancier was the King of Sweden, who owned Ch. Pang. Then too, there was Lady Halifax, who was the wife of the British ambassador to Washington and the first President of the British Elkhound Society.

That famous Alaskan musher, Arthur Walden, owned Elkhounds. He said that pound for pound they would out-pull any other dogs, provided that the snow was not too deep for the

Elkhound's short legs. A Maine race driver stated that his best dog was an Elkhound fifteen pounds lighter than the others.

The versatility of the breed is further emphasized by the fact that it can serve equally well hunting small game such as pheasants or big game such as bear. A dog of Boyesen's breeding was credited with 72 Cougars in two seasons of hunting in Washington. In fact, the Elkhound is ideally suited for this work, because he is the result of hundreds of generations of selective breeding by Mother Nature herself.

It is not only as a hunter, but also as a guard and a house-dog that this inhabitant of the North endears himself to his owners. An appropriate slogan appeared in *Dog World,* April, 1928, as an advertisement of the Norsk Dyrehund, "The Great Family Utility Dog of Today."

The Norwegian Elkhound Association of America began informally about 1930. Four years later there were four breeder members and nine other members. Total membership the next year was 25, including an honorary member, none other Johnny Aarflot, the noted Norwegian breeder of Elkhounds. On May 25, 1935, the Association adopted the British breed standard for the Norwegian Elkhound. This was superseded on November 12, 1935, by the official standard of Norway. The latter was translated into English by Aarflot. Some of the first officers of the Association were: Bayard Boyesen, W. Scott Cluett, Rex Cole, Amory Coolidge, Bradley Martin, A. Wells Peck, Lawrence Litchfield, Jr., and Thomas H. White.

Many of the early Norwegian pedigrees of Elkhounds are somewhat confusing in that there were no less than eight Frams, twenty Fins, six Finns, and goodness knows how many Bamses. Evidently the bloodlines of Skrub av Glitre, Burmann, and Bjonn were much sought after. At least a dozen progeny of Skrub were imported, of which three became American champions. Eight imports were sired by Burmann and ten by Bjonn. No less than 119 Elkhounds were imported prior to 1940, the high in annual importations being 20 dogs in 1933. This, of course, provided a great variety of type and bloodlines for the foundation stock in America.

All of the four imports sired by the English dog Krans finished their American championships: Flink of the Holm, Patsy of the Holm, Marko of the Holm, and Fourwents Brighde. Flink is credited with three Balmacaan champions in one litter from Patsy.

Ch. Brodd II av Elglia, Skrubb of Green Meadow, Ch. Marko of the Holm, and Ch. Martin of the Hollow. Owned by Green Meadow Kennels of Massachusetts.

George A. Cluett's Marko sired three Halfred champions from Thomas H. White's imported Norwegian Champion Saga av Elglia. Saga herself was the dam of six champions. She had acquired 14 points toward an American championship when she was lost. The famous English sire, Fourwents Frodi, owned by Miss F. J. Esdaile, was represented in the United States by several Fourwents champions.

Ch. Martin of the Hollow, bred by Mrs. L. F. G. Powys-Lybbe, England, and owned by Green Meadow Kennels, Mass.

Ch. Anna of the Hollow, bred by Mrs. L. F. G. Powys-Lybbe, England and owned by Gerd Berbom, Norway.

The Green Meadow Kennels of W. Scott Cluett and his sisters, Edith and Florence, were situated in the picturesque Green Mountains at Williamstown, Massachusetts. In the late thirties they housed two dozen Elkhounds, including the following seven champions:

Ch. Brodd II av Elglia (dog) A-70426
Ch. Fourwents Brighde (bitch) 955081
Ch. Jerv av Elglia (dog) A-145319
Ch. Marka of the Holm (bitch) 899229
Ch. Marko of the Holm (dog) 899228
Ch. Martin of the Hollow (dog) 955082
Ch. Sonja av Vindsval (bitch) 846488

All were imported except Sonja. Brodd II and his brother Jerv had moose-hunting records in Norway. Brodd II was Best of Breed three times at Westminster and again at Morris and Essex. Although he was not a large dog (19 inches at the shoulder), he was very stylish and well-proportioned. Apparently he did not sire any champions.

One of the great producing sires in American Elkhound history was Ch. Martin of the Hollow, bred by Mrs. L. F. G. Powys-Lybbe, England. He produced ten champions, then a record for the breed. They were from seven bitches. Robert P. Koenig, Zionsville, Indiana, bred his Viki of Halfred and his Paal's Girl of Lindvangen to Martin, thus producing five Kongsberg champions. From the latter mating came Ch. Olaf av Kongsberg, A-428308, who was almost as good a producer as his sire; according to the record, Olaf sired nine champions. Not far behind, with eight champions was Olaf's half brother, Rolf of Lindvangen, A-558499, bred by Priscilla S. Litchfield, New Canaan, Connecticut. Another son of Martin was Joseph W. Beatman's Ch. Green Meadow Marco Polo, A-48298. The Balmacaan Kennels and the Green Meadow Kennels imported two of Martin's sons from England that became American champions. It is evident that Ch. Martin of the Hollow was a prepotent sire and that the foundation stock of the Elkhound in America was greatly influenced by his bloodlines. He was described as a very good, dark-eyed dog with nice body and feet, but a little long, and carrying a bit of brush on his tail.

Oliver F. Holden, Chester, Connecticut, imported a number of Elglia dogs from Johnny Aarflot. Wade Stevenson brought over Ch.

Stavsetras Lars, A-284033, from Charles Stavseth, Norway. About the same time the Bradley Martins, Westburg, New York, purchased dogs in England and Norway for their Thistleton Kennels, the name of which was later changed to Balmacaan.

As early as 1927, Lawrence Litchfield, Jr. New Canaan Connecticut, his wife, and his daughters became interested in the breed. He served as Secretary and then as President of the Norwegian Elkhound Association of America for many years. Later he became vice-president of Alcoa, and moved to Pittsburgh. As a breed judge, his services were much in demand. His Lindvangen suffix figures in the pedigrees of more than twenty champions, the best known of which are:

Ch. Rolf of Lindvangen (dog), A-558499
Ch. Paal's Son of Lindvangen (dog), A-316133
Ch. Leif av Lindvangen (dog), A-159874
Ch. Hanna of Lindvangen (bitch), A-982434
Ch. Linda of Lindvangen (bitch), A-24455
Ch. Helga av Lindvangen (bitch), A-230075
Ch. Lova of Lindvangen (bitch), A-955175
Ch. Thor of Lindvangen (dog), A-582743

Probably the longest Elkhound name on record was carried by one of Litchfield's dogs, Gersky Kimmobroddsdatter, A-135061. Mr. Litchfield remained a staunch friend of the breed until his death in 1967.

The Kettle Cove Kennels of Amory Coolidge, Magnolia, Massachusetts, supplied breeding stock to many of the kennels starting in the thirties. Among them were the Romsdal Kennels of Miss Alice O'Connell, Minneapolis, Minnesota. From Ch. Kettle Cove Cora, 850138, came her Ch. Ragnhilde av Romsdal, A-10195, the first Elkhound to obtain the Companion Dog (C.D.) title in an obedience trial. A kennelmate, Ch. Rurig av Romsdal C.D. A-68913, completed his bench championship in four consecutive shows within nine days and at less than one year of age. Ragnhilde was the dam of four champions, including Miriam Phillips' and Dorothy Pile's Ch. Tronheim av Joywood, Olav Wallo's Ch. Graydal av Joywood, and Barbara Thayer's Ch. Raerta av Romsdal and her Ch. Popover of Stonewall.

In 1937, A. Wells Peck (of the internationally famous women's stores, Peck and Peck) and his wife, Catherine, imported Ch.

Ch. Rurig av Romsdal and Ch. Ragnhilde av Romsdal. Owned by Miss
Alice O'Connell.

Ch. Bluff, Kettle Cove Valma, and Ch. Thormin of Grey Dawn.

Fourwents Paal from England to head their Westview Kennel at Litchfield, Connecticut. Paal became the sire of five champions.

In 1941, Mr. and Mrs. Peck changed their kennel name to Pitch Road. It has continued to the present day as one of the longest-established and most distinguished in American dogdom.

Pitch Road has made some of the most notable Norwegian Elkhound importations to this country, including Ch. Koltorpets Paff from Sweden, Ch. Carro of Ardmere from England, and the celebrated Norwegian-Swedish-Canadian-American Champion Tortasen's Bjonn II from Dr. Jasper Hallingby in Norway. Bjonn was the first Norwegian Elkhound to win the prestigious Hound Group at Westminster. Whelped in 1952, by Ch. Bamse ex Ch. Moa, he was bred by Jacob Holseng, and was an official stud dog of Norway before his exportation. He was used extensively for breeding in America and has produced an impressive line of handsome Elkhounds that include Best in Show winners.

In recent years, the Pecks have also imported some young stock from Norway. How many champions they have bred and raised in over thirty years, I would not know, but it must be an impressive collection. I suspect that having a record number of champions is not too important to the Pecks—their concern is for the betterment of the breed. For their continued interest in the National Dog of Norway, Mr. and Mrs. Peck have received many awards, both from America and Norway. Mr. Peck has for years been the Norwegian Elkhound Association of America's delegate to the American Kennel Club.

After judging the Elkhounds at the 1940 Morris and Essex show, Bayard Boyesen said, "There is in all breeds of animals an undefinable quality that marks out the great from the excellent or merely correct. Ch. Binne av Skromtefjell fairly teems with this quality. It might be said that her tail could be more central and that her hind gait could be a bit wider; but this bitch combines in rare degree perfect type and exquisite finish with the most solid substance." He also observed "The Elkhound is a dog without extremes." Boyesen had to retire from dog activities because of a heart ailment, and his Vindsval Kennels, a landmark for twenty years, was dispersed. He died August 7, 1944.

Other kennels that were discontinued permanently or temporarily during the war were: Kettle Cove, Green Meadow,

Ch. Carro of Ardmere, owned by Pitch Road Kennels.

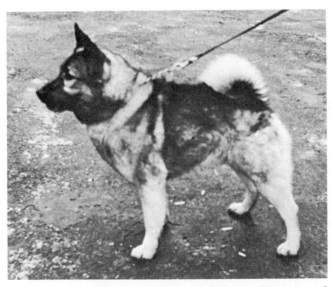

Ch. Tortassen's Bjonn II, bred by P. J. Holseng (Norway), and
owned by Pitch Road Kennels.

Balmacaan, Thistleton, and Seven League.

Robert P. Koenig, of Kongsberg fame, who became a major in the A.A.F., sold Ch. Olaf av Kongsberg, A-428308, and Ch. Marcia av Kongsberg, A-428314, to Floyd R. and J. Blanche Harding, South Bend, Indiana, who have maintained the strain that started with imported Ch. Martin of the Hollow and imported Marko of the Holm. They are the breeders of Ch. Olaf av Kongsberg III.

Joseph W. Beatman, later an enthusiastic Secretary of the Norwegian Elkhound Association of America, supervised the training of dogs for the Coast Guard in World War II. At first Elkhounds were accepted for Dogs for Defense and some were sent to the Canal Zone, but later only bigger dogs were enlisted. Some Elkhounds were trained as search and rescue dogs whose task it was to locate injured persons and signal their whereabouts by staying with the victim and barking. The Elkhound's method of hunting doubtless suited him well to this task.

Active in Norwegian Elkhound circles from 1932 to 1951 were Mr. and Mrs. Thomas H. White, Cleveland Heights, Ohio. In 1936, Mr. White imported that famous Norwegian Champion, Saga av Elglia, A-45983, who had three times won the coveted "Prize of Honor" of the Norsk Kennel Klub. This bitch possessed a strong head, heavy bone, tight tail, and beautiful light gray color, and was the producer of six champions.

Because Mr. White was also interested in the Elkhound as a hunter, he shipped one of his breeding to a government hunter in Montana; this dog was used for hunting mountain lions in a Grant-land Rice "Sportlight." Another of Mr. White's Halfred dogs at 17 years of age was donated to Cornell Research Department for experiments in the feeding of aged dogs.

In his capacity as Secretary of the parent club, Mr. White did much to promote the Elkhound. It was a great shock to the fancy when his private plane crashed in the Potomac River on October 26, 1951, carrying him, his wife, and his daughter-in-law to their untimely deaths. They were on their way to have luncheon with General George Marshall, who had just been given an Elkhound puppy named "Nato" by the high school children of Norway in appreciation for his part in the North Atlantic Treaty Organization.

Another breeder-judge who started with Elkhounds in the thirties is George Brooks Jr. (Vadstena Kennels,) Scranton, Pennsylvania.

Ch. Fourwents Paal, owned by Mr. and
Mrs. A. Wells Peck.

He judged the breed twice at Westminster and once at Morris and
Essex. During 1951 and 1952, he was President of the Norwegian
Elkhound Association of America. His best known dogs were Ch.
Christian of Northway, 845979, and Christian of Vadstena II, A-
786411. The latter, who sired four champions, was killed by an
automobile at 12 years of age. One of his offspring was Ch. Bjorn
Ringessen of Stonewall (dog), H-24962, who sired five champions

Ch. Paal's Son of Lindvangen, owned by Mr.
and Mrs. A. Wells Peck.

and was owned by Dr. Margaret Ascher Beach (Ringstead Kennels), Forestville, Connecticut, a veterinarian.

On her return from a European trip, Dr. Beach brought back Sorvangens Sonja (bitch), H-144750, which she obtained from Reidar Stromme in Norway. Dr. Beach donated one of her dogs to Seeing Eye, Inc., as a guide to a blind young woman. She was the breeder of Ch. Bjorgulf Sigurdssen (dog), A-854708, a great show dog with 9 Group wins and 19 Group placings, owned by the late Joseph W. Beatman of New York City. The late Evelyn Beatman and Bjorgulf made a lovely exhibit in the show ring, because she was an excellent handler and the dog a beautiful mover. Other Elkhounds to win Best in the Hound Group prior to 1952 include Ch. Binne av Glitre, Ch. Stavsetras Lars, Ch. Thor av Lindvangen, Ch. Tronheim av Joywood, Ch. Vingo of Inverailort, Ch. Gard of Pitch Road, Ch. Thorwald of Kongsberg, Ch. Torfinn av Runefjell, Ch. Bjorn Ringessen of Stonewall, Ch. Sigurd av Roughacres, Ch. Dyre Vaa Trim, Ch. Fraboo, Ch. Gray Rock av Pomfret, Kari's Bena, Rugg av Runefjell, and Ch. Trond III.

Harold T. Schnurer, of the prominent Carolyn-Schnurer women's wear firm, imported Ch. Greta of the Holm from England. The well-known dogs of his kennel included Ch. Mr. Peck of Pitch Road and Ch. Mrs. Peck of Flag Point. Mr. Schnurer was secretary of the Norwegian Elkhound Association of America, parent club of the breed, for a time.

Mrs. Susan D. Phillips, present president of the parent club, has for many years produced Elkhounds of consistently fine type at her small Pomfret Kennels in South Royalton, Vermont. Mrs. Phillips served previously as secretary, as treasurer, and as editor of the Newsletter for the club.

In 1950, Pomfret Norwegian Elkhounds swept the breed honors at Morris and Essex show, taking Best of Breed, Best of Winners, Winners Dog, Reserve Winners Dog, and Winners Bitch ribbons.

In 1962, at the first National Specialty Show sponsored by the parent club, held in conjunction with the International Kennel Club of Chicago all-breed show, and with Johnny Aarflot of Norway judging, Mrs. Phillips' Ch. Gladjac Royal Oslo was judged Best of Breed, and then went on to the Best in Show award. Winners Dog was a son of Royal Oslo, Frosti of Pomfret, who finished his championship at this show.

Ch. Arctic Storm of Pomfret pictured winning the second
National Norwegian Elkhound Specialty (122 entires), at
San Francisco in 1965, under judge Miss Gerd Berbom.
Handled by breeder, Mrs. Susan D. Phillips. Owned by
Doris Gustafson.

In 1965, at the second National Specialty Show sponsored by the
NEAA, held in conjunction with the Golden Gate Kennel Club
show at San Francisco, Arctic Storm of Pomfret—another son of
Royal Oslo, was placed Best of Breed by Gerd Berbom of Norway,
and went on to win the Group. Arctic Storm, owned by Doris
Gustafson, was handled by his breeder, Mrs. Phillips.

To return to doings in the 1950's, Mrs. H. H. Smertenko bred a
fine litter of Nordkyn dogs, sired by Ch. Carro of Ardmere. Ch. Solv
Prinz Narvikwood av Skromtefjell, H-232098, was purchased by
Francis L. Wood (Narvikwood Kennels) of Bath, New York, from
Sven Mjearum, Norway. Mrs. Wood also owned Ch. Elmwood Finn
av Vaker Lund, purchased from the Terrelys of Canada, who had

themselves purchased him from Sweden. Other imports of the time from Norway were Ch. Gaupa av Tallo (bitch), H-205150 and Ch. Skrub II av Skromtefjell (dog), H-205149, brought over by L. J. Yettergaard (Avogaard Kennels) of Fallbrook, California in 1951. Mr. Yettergaard, who was born in Norway, spent many years at sea as a master mariner, and when he retired, there was no question as to what breed of dog he wanted to own—it had to be the National Dog of his native land. He also purchased Ch. Paal av Jarlsberg from Earl Brunsvold.

Not long after, Martha M. Durmer imported Ch. Rugg (dog), H-218419 and Oro av Tallo (bitch), H-223726 from Norway.

Between 1938 and 1955, 78 Elkhounds were awarded the C.D. (Companion Dog) degree at Obedience trials. Ten obtained C.D.X. (Companion Dog Excellent), but only two received U.D. (Utility Dog). Mrs. Adele G. Koopman, Newton Highlands, Mass. had four dogs with C.D. titles, including Ch. Oleff and Ch. Fourwents Moln. A Dog World award of Canine Distinction was presented to 16-year-old Patricia Vincent, Norfolk, Virginia, when her Ch. Ulf's Madam Helga won her C.D. degree in three trials in 1952. (We shall hear more of Miss Vincent further on in this chapter.) Dr. R. A. Allen of Adrian, Michigan received a similar award when his Eric av Upsala won a C.D. in three shows in 1954.

The Kviltorp Kennels of Mrs. Robert J. Stuwe, Centerline, Michigan, were named after her father's home in Trondheim, Norway, high on a hill overlooking the city. The Stuwes, who had bred Pomeranians in the 1930's, owned the Elkhounds, Ch. Martin av Kviltorp, Ch. Torvald av Kviltorp, and Runefjell Lille Mor.

The late Barbara Thayer Hall, of Stonewall fame, owned Elkhounds beginning in 1934. Of the dozens of Stonewall champions, the greatest was probably Ch. Boreas of Stonewall, who died in 1954 at 15 years of age. He was a large, majestic, medium-gray dog with a marvelous disposition, and was a good producer, siring four champions. Mrs. Hall had shown some red Elkhounds at Westminster in 1941.

The Thorslands of Ithaca, New York, imported several Elkhounds including Camla of Ardmere from Scotland, Ch. Listuas Bamsi from Norway, and Ch. Skall-Trixi from Sweden. Trixi was the dam of four Dyre Vaa champions.

Ch. Skrub II av Skromtefjell, bred by Sven
Mjearum, and owned by Avogaard Kennels in
California.

Ch. Gaupa av Tallo, pictured in 1950 at 1 year
of age. Bred by Olav Campbell, and owned by
Avogaard Kennels in California.

Mrs. Nellie B. Wood Hilsmier of Fort Wayne, Indiana, first owned Chows, but is better known today for the many Borzoi and Elkhound champions that have come from her Woodhill Kennels. Her Ch. Nordic av Woodhill and Ch. Vika av Woodhill were the first Elkhounds to own both American and Canadian championships. Mrs. Hilsmier also owned a sister to Vika, Ch. Ola av Zimmies, who established a record at the time as the dam of ten champions. Seven of these were from the half-brother and sister matings of Ola to Nordic, and the other three were from the mating of Ola to her grandson, Ch. Rugg av Woodhill. These dogs were linebred to the English import Ch. Martin of the Hollow through Ch. Olaf av Kongsberg and Ch. Marcia av Kongsberg.

Luther M. Tollefsrud (Rokheim Kennels), Minneapolis, a former director of the parent club, started with Elkhounds in 1950. He obtained Ch. Rokk av Runefjell (Trygg av Skromtefjell ex Ch. Stella) from Olav Wallo, and Ch. Precilla av Jarlsberg (Ch. Steig av Jarlsberg ex Runa av Jarlsberg) from Earl Brunsvold. The two, both of whom had been imported in utero, won top honors at the Minnesota Specialty shows in 1954 and 1955.

Among the foremost Norwegian Elkhounds of the 1950's was Ch. Trond III, owned by Norman T. Fuhlrodt of Des Moines. He was the winner of 16 Group Firsts. Another top dog of the decade was Ch. Tari's Haakon, C.D., a son of imported Ch. Fourwents Rugg av Aalesund, owned by Florence H. Palmer. Haakon was Best of Breed at Westminster three years in succession, at Chicago International two consecutive years, and at Morris and Essex once. His sister, Ch. Tari's Binnie, finished her championship early.

Mrs. Palmer is owner of the famous Torvallen Kennels in New Hampshire. For many years, she has most capably served as treasurer for the Norwegian Elkhound Association of America. Her energies and abilities have contributed to the success of the NEAA with such projects as the annual financial contribution to the Cornell Institute of Veterinary Research, and the NEAA committee to study the problem of Progressive Retinal Atrophy in the breed. Ch. Torvallen Frosti, bred by Mrs. Palmer, has recently been a consistent winner on the New England show circuits.

Miss Elsie Healey of Litchfield, Connecticut is also a breeder whose dedication to the welfare of the breed deserves recognition. Breeder of such noteworthy champions as Ch. Kay's Kima of

Ch. Blakken av Norskfjell, bred and owned
by L. M. Tollefsrud.

Dal-Gard Viking, Ch. Tara's Binnie, Ch. Tari's Thorwald,
and Ch. Tari's Haakson, owned by Florence Palmer.

Dragondell and Ch. Leif of Dragondell, C.D.X., T.D. (owned by the Honorable William A. Timbers), Miss Healey has been devoting her full attention to the housing, care, breeding and raising of the Progressive Retinal Atrophy test litter of Elkhounds, for the research work conducted by Dr. D. Cogan of the Howe Eye Clinic, Boston. The breed owes her a debt of gratitude for this unselfish work.

The Honorable William A. Timbers, chief U.S. District judge in Connecticut, has served as president of the Norwegian Elkhound Association of America. The tremendous impact registered by his dog, Ch. Leif of Dragondell, C.D.X., T.D., the only Elkhound champion to ever acquire Tracking degree, is told in the chapter on Norwegian Elkhound personality in this book. Leif's descendants, Leiflet and Oslet, frequently accompany the judge to court sessions, and an order to "Clear the court!" does not include them. Judge Timbers was recently elected a director of the American Kennel Club, after having served several years as head of one of the AKC trial boards.

Mrs. Edna Mae Bieber, owner of the Thornbeck Kennels in Douglassville, Pa. is a breeder-judge who has served the Norwegian Elkhound well. For several years, her columns in the official American Kennel Club publication, *Pure-bred Dogs,* have provided useful and informative reading for Elkhound enthusiasts. Her courageous efforts to warn breeders of the presence of Progressive Retinal Atrophy in the breed, and contributions to research in this area, are especially to be commended. Her efforts, along with those of Miss Healey, have provided much information. Mrs. Bieber has judged the breed at several Specialties in recent years. The roll-call of Thornbeck champions includes: Ch. Thornbeck Lon of Stonewall, Ch. Thornbeck Tyra, Ch. Thornbeck Tristram and Ch. Thornbeck Trygvason.

As we come closer to a survey of the current scene, a note of explanation is in order. The ranks of Norwegian Elkhound breeders have grown considerably in recent years. In giving a skimming picture of the current national scene, as I aim to do in the paragraphs ahead, I appreciate that I may omit or seemingly slight some kennels. Believe me, it is not intentional. The reports must necessarily be less detailed than that of the pioneer kennels—the story has just gotten to be too big. Nor should any inference be

A Pomfret trio. Ch. Oh So Good of Pomfret, Ch. Karen of Pomfret, and Ch. Gray Rock of Pomfret.

Ch. Stella. Bred by H. Berg, Norway, and owned by Runefjell Kennels.

Dyre Vaa Karen II with litter of 14 pups (at age of two weeks). Sire was Ch. Prins Fron of Maple Leaf, C.D. Owned by Mrs. Borger Lien.

drawn from either the order in which the kennels are presented, or the amount of space given them. I will try to move across the country, telling first of the kennels in the Northwest, then California, then the Midwest and back to the East.

One of the most exciting areas of current activity in the breed is in the Northwest, and much of the credit for this must go to Mr. and Mrs. Borger O. Lien. Their kennel was a pioneer of the Norwegian Elkhound in this section of the country, and most of the Elkhound kennels here have Northgate strains in their pedigree. Now, after many years, the Liens have slowed down somewhat—there is no longer the hustle and bustle in their kennels that there was in bygone years. Most of the fine Elkhounds bred here have gone to happy hunting grounds, but the Liens will long be remembered as the trailblazers for the Elkhound in the Northwest.

In 1952, Mrs. Winston W. Scott of Seattle, Washington acquired the bitch that was to become Ch. Lady Kazana of Greenwood, foundation for a leading kennel of its day—the Greenwood Kennels. Lady Kazana was sired by Napoleon of Northgate, a fine dog purchased by Mrs. Lien from a California kennel, and her dam was Lady Tina, bred by Mrs. Lien in her Northgate Kennels and owned by a Mrs. Bryant of Mercer Island, Washington. Lady Kazana was never beaten in the ring by a female. (Of course there wasn't the competition in those days that we have now, but nevertheless, she was a magnificent bitch.) As a producer, she was equally outstanding. Two of her descendants became Best in Show winners (Ch. Baard of Greenwood and Lady Linda of Greenwood), making the Greenwood Kennels the first American kennel to produce two Norwegian Elkhound Best in Show winners. Two littermate offspring not only made championships in quick order, but also acquired the top Obedience degree, Utility Dog (U.D.) with high scores. These were Ch. Just Torvald That's All, U.D. (owned by Louis H. Priner) and Am. & Can. Ch. Norska of Greenwood, Am. & Can. U.D. (owned by Lili P. Fowler). The Greenwood bloodlines provided foundation stock for several kennels that are now among the tops in the breed.

Mrs. Halvord Hoff, owner of the Keyport Kennels in Paulsboro, Washington, was born in Norway, so her love for Elkhounds is a natural one. She purchased her first Elkhound, Ch. Vicki, from Mrs. Lien. After owning Vicki for a while, she decided to add a male. She wrote to Peter Jakob Holseng in Norway, and bought a son of Ch. Bamse ex Ch. Moa. This dog, Am. & Can. Ch. Viking, Am. & Can. C.D., was to make as strong an impact on the breed in the Northwest as his brother, Int. Ch. Tortasen's Bjonn II, did in the East.

I am sure that no one will deny that Viking, whelped in 1954, is the key dog in the excellent quality of the Northwest Elkhound. His offspring include such famous dogs as Am. & Can. Ch. Wabeth's Gustav, Ch. Trygve of Keyport, Ch. Wabeth's Bjarne, Ch. Princess Moa of Keyport, and Ch. Ragnaar av Fowlerstad. The innumerable number of champion grandsons and granddaughters include Ch. Gus 'N Zorei's Etterman and Ch. Baard of Greenwood. Almost every Elkhound in the area can find Viking in its pedigree somewhere.

Also imported by Mrs. Hoff were Ch. Jennie of Skromtefjeld (from Norway) and Ravenstone Brand (from England). Current star, Ch. Mikkel of Keyport II, owned by Dr. and Mrs. Robert Indeglia of Minneapolis, is a grandson of Viking and Jennie. Mikkel finished his championship with three consecutive 5-point wins at age of ten months.

Deep in the evergreen woods at Auburn, Washington are the Wabeth Kennels, owned by Mr. and Mrs. Walter Moore. An ideal place to raise Norwegian Elkhounds, the woods provide shady and cool places for the dogs in hot weather, and protection in high wind and storms. The runs are large and open on a hillside, so there is plenty of room to exercise, to play, or to climb the hills. Here is the home of Am. & Can. Ch. Wabeth's Gustav, a five-time winner of Best in Show (three in the U.S. and two in Canada), and the producer of some very fine Elkhounds.

Lili Fowler's (Fowlerstad Kennels at Seattle Washington) first Elkhound was the afore-mentioned Lady Kazana of Greenwood daughter, Am. & Can. Ch. Norska of Greenwood, Am. & Can. U.D. Norska was a consistent winner of Best of Breed or Best of Opposite Sex. She had a tremendous personality. Mrs. Fowler often took her Elkhounds to children's hospitals, and the youngsters were particularly delighted with Norska's ability to solve problems in arithmetic, barking the correct number in answer to Lili's questions. (She barked according to given signals.) Norska was tragically killed by a hit-run driver.

Mrs. Fowler was very active in the Washington State Obedience

Ch. Lady Kazana of Greenwood, first Norwegian Elkhound
bitch to go Best in Show in America. Owners, Mr. and Mrs.
Winston Scott.

Am. & Can. Ch. Viking, Am. & Can. C.D., Norwegian import,
whelped 1954, one of the great sires of the breed. Owner, Mrs.
Halvord Hoff.

Club, and served as its president for two years. Her great Am. & Can. Ch. Ragnaar av Fowlerstad, Am. & Can. U.D. (obtained from Mrs. Halvord Hoff), was sire of Ch. Er-Sue Rikke av Fowlerstad, and grandfather of Ch. Dagne and Ch. Sunde—both of whom have high degrees in Obedience.

It is a coincidence that the city of Seattle has two Fowler families with show-going Elkhounds. Mr. and Mrs. Worth Fowler own Ch. Baard of Greenwood. Baard, a dog of good size, well-built with a proud carriage, was the fifth Elkhound in the United States to win Best in Show. He was shown extensively, and compiled a record that did much for the breed. It was his success that paved the way for Elkhound wins of the Group and Best in Show in the Northwest. Mr. Fowler served as president of the Norwegian Elkhound Association of America for two years.

To compete and hold your own in the tough Norwegian Elkhound competition in the state of Washington is no easy task, but Georgia M. Cole's Branstock Kennels has made a great success of it. It is not a large kennel establishment, but its Elkhounds are known from coast to coast. Ch. Norda Fylgie of Branstock was the nation's top Norwegian Elkhound bitch for 1965. Other famous winners include Ch. Branstock Joker Joe, a group winner and his sister, Ch. Branstock Silhouette (finished to championship at 10 months). Georgia Cole, together with Dr. Milo T. Harris owned Ch. Windy Cove's Rowdy Ringo—a foremost winning Elkhound of the mid-1960's.

On the way to the 1962 First National Specialty at Chicago, Thelma Heyworth—who with her husband Earl owns the Cedarstone Kennels in Spokane, Washington—came to my place for a visit. In her station wagon she had four handsome Elkhounds. They were all nice, but one little female especially sparkled. She was a bit on the small side, but very well put together. Her name was Cedarstone Zorei.

Judge at the Specialty was Johnny Aarflot from Norway. Little Zorei kept clearing one hurdle after another. Thelma Heyworth had driven over 2,000 miles just to get to the show, and I believe we were all pulling for the little trooper, Zorei, to get the Best Opposite ribbon. It was tough competition, but finally she did get the call, and I am sure that the 2,000 miles back to Spokane did not seem so far for Thelma.

Ch. Lady Karen of Greenwood, bred and owned by Mrs. Winston W. Scott.

Am. & Can. Ch. Baard of Greenwood. Bred by Mrs. Winston W. Scott, and owned by Mr. and Mrs. Worth Fowler.

Ch. Stor Glad of Greenwood, bred and owned by Mrs. Winston W. Scott.

75

Ch. Cedarstone's Irish Kaughphy and his Best in Show winning dam, Ch. Cedarstone's Zorei, bred and owned by Thelma J. Heyworth.

Zorei finished her championship with three 5-point wins, and after that won Best of Breed at Westminster, many Hound Groups, and a Best in Show at Mensona Kennel Club. What's more, she was dam of a Best in Show winner. Currently carrying on in her winning steps are Cedarstone Irish Kauphy and Zorei II.

In the Egersund Kennels of Terry and Linda Ege at Portland, Oregon, we find such notable Elkhounds as Am. & Can. Ch. Norsemen's Nord Nyal, Egersund's Tryg Tasjo and Heide av Egersund. From England they have imported English Ch. Gerda of Eskamere (Best of Breed at Crufts in 1967), by Eng. Ch. Musti of the Holm ex Eng. Ch. Solveig of Eskamere. The Eges are the editors of Arligg (*Aarlig* in Norwegian), an interesting annual Elkhound stud directory, illustrated with good pictures of many champions.

The Er-Sue Kennels (Edna Swift Asp and Mary C. Potter in Beaverton, Oregon) was founded on Greenwood stock. Though modest in size, it has produced an impressive array of champions that include Ch. Er-Sue D, Ch. Er-Sue Kjeere Ven of Greenwood,

Ch. Eiress av Cedarstone, a Group-winning bitch. Owned by Gladys and Guy Cutter.

Ch. Cedarstone's Vidungergutt, Group winner. Bred by Cedarstone Kennels.

Ch. Branstock's Highland Ladd, co-owned by Georgia M. Cole and Elizabeth Butler.

Ch. Norda's Fylgie of Branstock, owned by Georgia M. Cole.

Ch. Branstock's Highland Gus, owned by Mrs. Helen Tate Hermann.

Ch. Branstock's Joker Joe, owned by Georgia M. Cole.

Can. Ch. Sunde av Fowlerstad and Ch. Dagne av
Fowlerstad. Owned by Lili P. Fowler.

Am. & Can. Ch. Er-Sue Rikke av
Fowlerstad, Am. & Can. C.D. Bred by
Mary C. Potter. Owned by Lili P.
Fowler.

Can. Ch. Norsemen's Nord Nyal, at 13
mos. Owned by Mrs. Linda Ege.

Ch. Er-Sue Miss Wiant, Ch. Er-Sue Rikke av Fowlerstad, Ch. Er-Sue Spiger, Ch. Er-Sue's Tunka of Greenwood and Ch. Er-Sue Suzska.

There is a healthy continuing interest in the breed in the Northwest. Nicely on the way is the Kenne Acres Kennels of Steve and Judi Keenan in Bremerton, Washington. Their first Elkhound was Ch. Windy Cove Golly's Molly. Bred to Marie Peterson's Norwegian import, Ch. Windy Cove's Tass av Oftenasen, Molly has produced some fine offspring. A promising future seems also in store for the Vikesland Kennels of Anthony and Edan Wilson in Seattle. They have been carefully collecting good breeding stock, and are young and energetic.

Mr. and Mrs. Joe Peterson, and their son, started their Windy Cove Kennels in Spokane, Washington but moved to Atascadero, California, where it is now one of the largest Elkhound kennels in the West.

Windy Cove has always been a family project. They've set as their slogan "The Best in the West" and mean to make it a true one. Ch. Windy Cova Sweda Silva Slipa represents their 33rd champion in five generations.

From Norway, the Petersons have imported Ch. Windy Cove Tass av Oftenasen. Tass won two Specialty Bests in Show in 1968, and is sure to even further improve Windy Cove breeding stock. Windy Cove Mona av Oftenasen was imported early in 1968, and three months later won Best of Winners on to Best of Opposite Sex at the third National Specialty at Springfield, Mass., judged by Olav Campbell of Norway. The breezes of Windy Cove will blow strong across the Norwegian Elkhound show rings of the future.

Success began very early for another California transplant, Patricia Vincent Craige, who with her husband John, a veterinarian, owns the Vin-Melca Kennels at Monterey. Pat was only 13 years old (in 1949), and living in the East, when she acquired her first Norwegian Elkhound, a puppy that grew up to be the matriarch of her kennels, Ch. Ulf's Madam Helga, C.D. Helga was a combination of Stonewall and Lindvangen lines. We have already noted how Pat, at 16 years of age, received a Dog World Award of Canine Distinction, in honor of Helga's Obedience prowess.

Upon graduation from college, Pat purchased an 8-week-old puppy from the Pitch Road Kennels. This ball of fluff became the all-time top winning bitch of the breed, Ch. Vin-Melca's Rebel

Am. & Can. Ch. Wabeth's Brenda. Bred and owned by Walter and Elizabeth Moore.

Am. & Can. Ch. Wabeth's Jalmar, Canada's top winning Elkhound for 1967. Bred and owned by Walter and Elizabeth Moore.

Ch. Wabeth's Kia, first homebred champion of the Wabeth Kennels of Mr. and Mrs. Walter D. Moore.

Am. & Can. Ch. Wabeth's Gustav, one of the all-time show greats of the breed, with 5 Bests in Show (3 in U.S., 2 in Canada), and sire of more than a dozen champions. Bred and owned by Mr. and Mrs. Walter D. Moore, Wabeth Kennels.

Ch. Windy Coves Rowdy Ringo, Best in Show winner. Purchased as a pet, Ringo's spectacular show successes launched Georgia M. Cole's Branstock Kennels.

Ch. Windy Coves Silver Son, Winner of NEANC Outstanding Dog Award 1961, and of NEANC Stud Dog Award 1963. Owned by Gladys and Guy Cutter.

Ch. Vin-Melca's Howdy Rowdy, winner of 5 all-breed Bests in Show. Winner of the third National Specialty in 1968 under judge Olav Campbell of Norway. Sire of 5 champions in his first three litters. Owned by Dr. and Mrs. John E. Craige.

Rouser. The mating of Rebel Rouser with the Pecks' great import, Ch. Tortasen's Bjonn II in 1961 set Vin-Melca on course to the eminence it enjoys today. Three outstanding bitches came of this mating: Ch. Vin-Melca's Moa of Pitch Road (owned by the Pecks), dam of 7 champions; Ch. Vin-Melca's Rebel Cry, Best of Opposite Sex at the 1965 National Specialty under Miss Gerd Berbom of Norway; and Ch. Vin-Melca's Rebel Rouser, dam of 8 champions including Ch. Vin-Melca's Vickssen, a Best in Show winner and the Stud Dog winner at the 1968 Specialty.

The triumph of triumphs for the kennel came in 1968 when, at the Third National Specialty, held in Springfield, Massachusetts, judge Olav Campbell from Norway placed Ch. Vin-Melca's Howdy Rowdy to Best of Breed over an entry of 135, a salute to all American-bred Norwegian Elkhounds. Howdy Rowdy is establishing a record that may well make him the all-time show winner for the breed, and following right in his Best in Show footsteps is Ch. Vin-Melca's Vagabond (a Vickssen son). At the 1970 show, Vagabond became the first Norwegian Elkhound since Bjonn II to win the Group at Westminster (see page 58).

Ch. Vin-Melca's Rebel Rouser (1958–1965), one of the all-time great show winners of the breed, and an immortal producer. Owned by Vin-Melca Kennels.

Ch. Vin-Melca's Vickssen, all-breed and Specialty Best in Show winner. Sire of champions. Pictured with owner, Pat Vincent Craige.

The kennel name Vin-Melca ("the corny invention of a teenager") is derived from a merging of VIncent, her maiden name; MElody, a Cocker pet; and CAndy, call name of Madam Helga. A fine competitor, Mrs. Craige likes to show her Elkhounds against the best in the country, and is a good sport—win or lose.

There were very few Elkhounds in the area when the first dogs of the Highland Kennels at Hayward, California were being shown. In fact, it was hard to find six owners or breeders within a radius of 300 miles. But since that time, Elkhound interest in the West has advanced tremendously, and today this is one of the strongest areas for the breed in the country.

Daro's Charjer Boy, at 9½ mos. Owned by Mr. and Mrs. E. D. Philbrick, Jr.

Ch. Smokey av Lyncrest, owned by Mr. and Mrs. E. D. Philbrick, Jr.

Silverlance Dawn'n Sun's Jolly, owned by Philip A. Buscemi.

Highland Kennels, co-owned by Gladys and Guy Cutter with Craig Tangen, has been very important in this advance, adding much to the quality of the Elkhounds in California. The roll-call is long: Ch. Highland Branstock Renegade, Viking Ruff, Silver's Mikar, Silver's Ladic, Rhondi of Highland, and many more—all from Highland, and all champions. It seems that the "3 Musketeers"—Gladys, Guy and Craig—have done pretty well.

Rolling Hills Estate is a very exclusive place in Southern California, and here is where Helen Philbrick has her Lyncrest Kennels. It is not a large Elkhound establishment—only a few dogs, but handsome ones, well-groomed, well-guarded and loved. Ch. Smokey av Lyncrest and Black Bart's Silver Mist are the best known Lyncrest Elkhounds. If the Norwegian Elkhound in America had many homes like this, his future would be well-assured.

In another beautiful spot, on a hill overlooking the valley, the rolling landscape and large orchards at La Habra, California, Louis and Etta Schleimer have their home and La Habra Hills Kennels. From here have come many champions including Ch. Robretta of La Habra Hills, C.D., Ch. Guinivere of La Habra Hills, and many more. Ch. Thuse of La Habra Hills, although a young dog, has had some fine wins. He is owned by Janet and Stewart Warter of Huntington Beach, California.

Herbert and Marie Stahl have purchased an acre of land in a mountain setting in Santa Rosa, California. Their kennel name is Fjellbu (Mountain Cabin). From Norway they have imported the Elkhounds Lion (male) and Laika (female). Laika is of strong Kotofjell breeding. At Kotofjell, the emphasis is on moose hunting and Elkhound field trials. The Stahls are interested in producing and raising the best hunting-type Elkhounds.

Stan and Mary Jenkins, of the Vine Hill Kennels at Santa Rosa, California, have been interested in the breed for some time—not only for show, but also for the deer hunting they enjoyed with their Elkhound, Ch. Gra Tyr's Max of Jamaura (the only Elkhound champion in Northern California with the C.D. degree). California is one of the few states where a dog can be used on a deer hunt. Of course, Stan is extremely cautious as to where he hunts. He is always on guard for another hunter who might take Max for a coyote. Max is a good hunter—Stan has never come home empty-handed.

Stan sometimes goes on a hiking trip with one of the Elkhounds.

Ch. Actondale Tryglikk Dokke, owned by
Bill Hoops.

Tuftehuus Masa, owned by Ingvar Granhus.

Haar Vel's Rusken av Oftenasen. Bred by
Magna Aftret, Norway. Owned by Patricia V.
Craige and Velma B. Cook.

Stan carries the tent, sleeping bags, and his chow—the Elkhound has side packets strapped on, and carries his own food. This is one place where the Elkhounds have a wonderful life.

Robert and Jean Smolley of Tedondo Beach, California, also love camping out, and when they travel, the dogs are always along for protection and company. Their impressive Elkhounds, all of Crafdal breeding, include Crafdal Tryglik Trick, Crafdal Trygs Tiara, and Crafdal Tryglik Tamokkar. One night, on a trip, their male scented a bear close by, and Robert, hanging on to the leash, was pulled out of his sleeping bag and along the ground for some distance before he could stop the hunter.

A friend of the Smolleys tells an interesting story of how an Elkhound used to escort some children to school in Alaska. It seems that after a heavy snowstorm, a moose there took to walking on the plowed road the children used, and would not let them by. The Elkhound would pick a fight with the moose, and keep him occupied until the children had by-passed.

It is against the law to use dogs to hunt moose in Alaska because some years ago hunters used large packs of dogs that would chase and attack the moose, tearing it apart. This is regrettable, because this is one part of the world that would be ideal for the correct use of the Elkhound in hunting.

The purchase of a 10-week-old puppy in 1964 from Marie Peterson's Windy Cove Kennel turned out to be the start of the Silverlance Kennels, owned by Mr. and Mrs. Philip A. Buscemi of Portales, New Mexico. They named the puppy Folly. The Buscemis do not aim at having a large kennel. Mr. Buscemi is chairman of the biology department at Eastern New Mexico University, and their dogs are pure enjoyment for them. Not only have they collected a good share of show prizes, but they have had interesting experiences hunting bears in New Mexico with the Elkhounds. We wish the Buscemis the best of luck, for it is encouraging to find breeders that will keep the hunting instincts of the breed ever sharp.

Norwegian Elkhound interest is very strong in the Mid-west, too. When Miss Miriam Phillips purchased the Elkhounds from Miss Alice O'Connell's Romsdale Kennels in Minneapolis, she took over the oldest Norwegian Elkhound establishment in Minnesota. But Miss Phillips' Joywood Kennels, at Wayzata, Minnesota, has a long, illustrious history of its own. Ch. Trondheim av Jaywood, C. D., whelped in 1941, was the first Elkhound to win a Group in Minnesota, and but the fifth in the United States. Like his dam, Ch. Ranghilde av Romsdal, C.D. (the first Elkhound to win C.D. in the United States), "Trony" was an Obedience star, too. He was the sire of champions and obedience titlists, and the family strain he represented was a very important influence in the Midwest. Joywood Elkhound are especially celebrated for their hunting ability.

Miss Phillips was active in the organization of the Norwegian Elkhound Association of Minnesota, which became the first affiliate club to the paret Norwegian Elkhound Association of America. In connection with the 1959 specialty of the Minnesota club, at which Mrs. Kitty Heffer of England was the judge, there was held the first international Norwegian Elkhound Convention. A second convention was held in Santa Barbara, California in 1960.

These seminars are exactly what we need in this country, but I feel that they should be two-day gatherings, to allow plenty of time for informative discussion of the problems facing Norwegian Elkhound breeders, and that the foremost authorities of the breed should be in attendance.

In 1961, the Minnesota Breeder Division was formed with the announced objective of working for the production of strong and healthy Elkhounds of the hunting type.

We have already noted that Dr. and Mrs. Robert Indeglia launched their Tekdal Kennel, at Minneapolis, with purchase of Ch. Mikkel II of Keyport from Mrs. Halvord Hoff. A consistent Group placer, Mikkel shares company at Tekdal with such as Ch. Cedarstone's Vidundergutt and Ch. Tekla of Narvikwood.

Karen B. Elvin's Sangerud Kennels at Minneapolis is small, but has some mighty nice looking Elkhounds, principally of Jalsberg and Eunefjell strains. Ch. Lisa av of Sangerud is well known at the Minnesota shows. Mrs. Elvin is a fine writer, and her articles are often seen in the dog magazines, and in the Norwegian Elkhound Association of America's Newsletter. Look for her article on "Safeguarding the Norwegian Elkhound" that is in this book.

Mr. and Mrs. Arvid Erickson's Ericsgaard Kennels at Bloomington, Minnesota is home of Champions Ericsgaard Fram and Gyda av Vikingsholm. The Ericksons are particularly conscientious in seeing that the dogs they sell are well-adjusted to family life. From

n. Silver's Ladic of Highland, owned by
Mr. and Mrs. Clifford Johnson.

Ch. Lovdig Bjorn av Katrine Glen
("Little Bear"), owned by Katrine
Glen Kennels.

Gylefs Minun Hirviojakoira, bred and owned
by Mrs. Fred Calhoun.

Ch. Thorlief Haakonssen, owned by
Miss M. A. Endres.

Ch. Martin av Kviltorp, owned by
Mrs. R. J. Stuwe.

Ch. Torvallen Baron Greyfell, owned by
Ralph and Harry Schoonmaker.

the time he is four to five weeks old, each puppy is with the children, playing, running, and being carried about. Mrs. Erickson was a diligent worker with the Minnesota Breeder Division. She is author of the chapter on "Hunting Pheasants with Norwegian Elkhounds" that appears elsewhere in this book.

Nancy Torbet, of the Eidsvold Kennels in Mundelein, Illinois, acquired her first Norwegian Elkhound when she was 16 years old, and it became her first champion—Ch. Thor av Kongsberg. Others soon followed: Ch. Borreas av Eidsvold (sold to Dan McNab), Ch. Leif av Eidsvold, and Ch. Tassa av Eidsvold. Miss Torbet has imported a lovely female of excellent breeding, Noste av Kotofjell —sister of the great Driv av Kotofjell. We predict that it will not be long before many of the finest Elkhounds will be coming from Eidsvold.

When a Norwegian Elkhound is brought into the veterinary hospital where Mrs. Mildred Bitterman of Northbrook, Illinois works, you can be sure it receives special attention. Mrs. Bitterman owns Ch. Borg av Botsfjord, by Ch. Joywood's Rolvaag ex Lisa av Larsgaard. She is active in the Chicago Norwegian Elkhound Club, whose 35 members meet each month.

The Nordsvaal Kennels of Don and Bettie Duerksen of Wichita, Kansas, was launched with Ch. Fanabjorgs Bjorn av Bjorksyn, bred by the Lloyd Jacksons of St. Paul, and strong in Runefjell breeding. Nordsvaal Kennels has another promising youngster in Nordsvaal's Jaeger-Meister.

Few kennels of any breed can match the spectacular success of Crafdal Farms, established by Glenna and the late Bob Crafts at Stow, Ohio. Crafdal, registered in 1958, in less than a dozen years became the largest establishment for Norwegian Elkhounds in America, and set many all-time records for winning and breeding. A total of 190 Elkhounds bred at Crafdal were finished to championship in this period, 24 of them in the year of 1966 alone. Crafdal dogs have accounted for 5 all-breed Bests in Show, over 100 Group Firsts, and many Specialties.

Kingpin of the kennel has been Am. & Can. Ch. Trygvie Vikingsson. "Tryg," whelped June 1955, was one of the first litter bred by the Crafts. The top winning Elkhound in America throughout 1959, 1960, and 1961, he won 3 all-breed Bests in Show, 21 Group

The immortal Am. & Can. Ch. Trygvie Vikingsson, sire of
64 champions. Owned by Crafdal Kennels.

Two great Crafdal littermates—Ch. Crafdal Tryg
N Thors Rollo and Ch. Crafdal Tryg N Thors
Tufsen.

Ch. Crafdal Tryg N Thors Tufsen, at 13 months. Bred and owned by Crafdal Kennels.

Ch. Crafdal Tryg N Thors Rollo, bred and owned by Crafdal Kennels.

Am. & Can. Ch. Crafdal Thor Mhors Thunder, Best in Show winner. Bred and owned by Crafdal Kennels.

Firsts, and 10 Specialties. But it is as a sire that his immortality is assured: Tryg produced 64 champions.

Other Best in Show winners at Crafdal are Am. & Can. Ch. Crafdal Tryglik Turi ("Moose") and Am. & Can. Ch. Crafdal Thor Mhors Thunder. Presently, there are about 30 to 35 dogs enjoying a comfort that includes a pond in which to swim, and ten shaded acres in which to exercise. Mr. and Mrs. Crafts took special pride in handling their own dogs at the rings. Bob Crafts, who died in 1969, was an executive of the Goodyear Company, and had served as president of the Norwegian Elkhound Association of America for several years.

———————

Publisher's Note: The story of Norwegian Elkhound kennels in the Mid-west would hardly be complete without a report on the Runefjell Kennels, owned by our author. For this report, we are indebted to Brenda Ueland of Minneapolis.

The Runefjell Kennels lies in the middle of a 70-acre estate, on top of a high hill, with a sweeping view of Minneapolis and St. Paul skylines and the surrounding territories. It is located in the city of Bloomington (80,000 population), but only 9 miles from downtown Minneapolis. It is a place where the wilderness still whispers: where deer, beaver, raccoon, and fox are welcome free-loaders, and where birds of all sizes and colors wing above.

Olav Wallo learned to hunt the moose with Elkhounds in his native Norway. He first came to the United States in 1922, liked the country and people, and stayed. In 1946, he returned to Norway for a hunting holiday, and found some excellent Elkhounds. In 1949, he imported Ch. Stella, in whelp to the handsome Trygg av Skromtefjell. Two years later, he imported Ch. Fjeldheims Tito, one of the most famous ever sold out of Norway. From Tito's and Stella's bloodline have come 18 of the 30 Runefjell champions.

The Runefjell motto is "Honor, protect, and improve the breed," and it has been lived up to in every way. The kennels does not advertise, but there is a constant call for its puppies. As a rule, no puppies are sold before the age of four to six months, and the buyer

Best in Show winning team: Ch. Runefjell Gunar, Ch. Runefjell Dagney, Ch. Isabell av Runefjell, and Ch. Sigred av Runefjell.

Ch. Fjeldheims Tito, bred by L. Cappelen Smith (Norway) and owned by Olav Wallo.

is told all the puppy's faults as well as its good points. In this way, Olav Wallo has made friends of his customers all over the country.

A unique homecoming was celebrated in October 1957, when 29 dogs of Runefjell strain were brought back from near and far to be shown under judge William Thompson. A more handsome group of dogs would be hard to find. The lunch prepared and served by Mrs. Wallo and Mrs. Earl Brunsvold was something special—a real treat, especially for those who had never before tasted moose, deer, antelope and bear meat. It was a day that both host and guest will treasure for a long time.

Mr. Wallo is a member of six kennel clubs in different countries, and has for nine years been an officer of the Minneapolis Kennel Club (four years as treasurer). He promoted the first International Norwegian Elkhound Convention in Minneapolis in 1959, and appeared on the program of the Second Convention in Santa Barbara, California in 1960.

———————

Miss Doris H. Phillips, owner of the Elkins Kennels in Elkins, New Hampshire, has been the secretary of the Norwegian Elkhound Association of America for many years—and has done a masterful job.

The Elkhounds of Elkins include Ch. Aija av Pitch Road, Ch. Aija's Kearsarge of Elkins, Ch. Aija's Fjell of Elkins, and Ch. Aija's Jente of Elkins. For the convenience of their owner, and the pleasure of the dogs themselves, they have free access to their owner's home from their adjoining fenced yard. Her concern is with quality, rather than quantity. For the welfare of the Elkhound, let us hope that we have many of this type of kennel in our wonderful country.

Nancy Swanson (of the Norskogen Kennels in Andover, New Jersey) started to breed and show Norwegian Elkhounds in the early 1960's. Her first champion, Ch. Crafdal Trygs Glen, a handsome dog, made quite a name for himself in the East.

Miss Swanson is also making quite a name for herself as a historian of the breed. She has spent hours in the American Kennel Club offices collecting material and history on the breed. She has complete show records from 1946 to the present, and a tabulation of

Ch. Anastasia of Vine Hill, bred by Mary
O. Jenkins, and owned by Herb and Marie
Stahl.

Ch. Bojen of Trodheim, owned by Janet
Feltis.

all American Kennel Club Elkhound champions, with their sires and dams. It is heartwarming to know that we have some people in this country who have such interest and love for the breed, and the ability, to collect and preserve information for those who will follow.

The Fran-Van Kennels of Mrs. Louis Francoiose and Mrs. Charles Van Vleet of Nutley, New Jersey, is another where the emphasis is on quality, not quantity. It is not necessary to have a large kennel to produce good Elkhounds. Often, it seems, the best Elkhounds come from the small kennels. The breeding at Fran-Van is built on Crafdal, Pitch Road and Windy Cove bloodlines, and Ch. Tortasen Bjonn II has been the principal producer. In their kennel is to be found Takks Varg av Fran-Van, Tripps Rontu av Fran-Van, and of course, Ch. Tusen Takk av Fran-Van. Fran-Van Elkhounds have been seen often on television, and as models in the pages of Vogue.

Katrine Glen, which in Gaelic means "beautiful valley," is the home of the Elkhounds of Mr. and Mrs. Henry Glasgow. The mating of their first female, Ch. Leydig, to Bern av Vikingsholm, produced eight champions from one litter.

After retiring in 1954, Mr. Glasgow adopted the breeding of Elkhounds as a full-time hobby, and has interested Virginia Polytechnic Institute in a genetic study of the Elkhound and his breeding program.

The Glasgows have in their kennel Ch. Bamse av Oftenasen and Heidi VII from Sweden. The Glasgows will not breed any dogs of their own until they have been checked for retinal atrophy, x-rayed for hip dysplasia, wormed, and found to be in good physical condition. They likewise will not accept any female for breeding unless the above procedure has been followed, and there is a veterinarian's statement to that effect.

At the Blafjell Kennels, owned by Mr. and Mrs. Floyd Cox of Vinton, Virginia, the Elkhounds have 100 acres of farmland and woods in which to run and play. (Blafjell in Norwegian means Blue Mountain). Nevertheless, the Coxes are not interested in having a large kennel with lots of dogs, but prefer to concentrate on a few, but good ones.

Bern av Blafjell, Winners Dog in the Norwegian Elkhound Specialty at Goshen, was shot and killed by two boys—a great tragedy for the Coxes. They have imported Vakker Lunds Bjarni from Canada. And from Norway, they have imported Judy av Kotofjell, a sister of famous Driv av Kotofjell, and daughter of the producer of outstanding Elkhounds, Lotte av Kotofjell.

Mr. and Mrs. Jim Pederson have a few years of experience in Elkhound breeding, and have now purchased some land in Scandia, Minn. for larger runs and more room. They have come to the conclusion that a healthy Elkhound must have acres for running and playing.

Ch. Bamse av Oftenasen. Bred by Magne Aftret, Norway, and owned by Katrine Glen Kennels.

Ch. Fort Knox av Katrine Glen, C.D., owned by Katrine Glen Kennels.

Six puppies out of Leydig being shown in competition. Bred by Mr. and Mrs. Henry M. Glasgow.

101

Mr. and Mrs. William Kinsley, of Willsboro, New York, are started with Ch. Crafals Trygs Trykka, exceptional in personality. New to Elkhound breeding, but seemingly sure to be heard from are Mr. and Mrs. Victor Pinheiro and Mr. and Mrs. John Henschel of Minneapolis. The enthusiasm for the breed continues to grow and grow.

In the latter half of the 1960's new faces have appeared at shows throughout the country and new interest in the Elkhound is evident. In the Northwest, Mr. and Mrs. John Murphy, Mr. and Mrs. Steve Keenan and others have taken up the vacancies left by the passing of such dedicated Elkhounders as Violet Jones and Laura Hobson.

In California, Bev and Oscar Ricci, the Russel Guthries and Carmen Streif have become active in the work of the Northern California Elkhound Club. The Southern California club has found willing workers for the breed in Marilyn and Tom Braly, Freeman and Betty Claus and the John Hoffmans. Dogs owned and bred by these newcomers are beginning to do their share of winning at the Califoria shows.

In Colorado, the Valdemar Kennels of Jack Hack have begun to produce consistent winners and a nucleus of interested owners exists in that territory.

In Minnesota, new and eager faces appearing at the shows and in club work are Jack and Sharon Henschel and Victor and Carol Pinheiro.

Two new regional Elkhound clubs have recently been formed. In the New Jersey area, the Garden State Norwegian Elkhound Club is undertaking many useful projects. Among its willing workers are Mr. and Mrs. William Hoops, Miss Margaret Kampish, Nancy Swanson, and Richard Gamsby. The Norwegian Elkhound Club of South Florida was formed through the efforts of Richard Deimel, Mr. and Mrs. Andy Guffy and Mrs. Joan Conklin. Continued efforts of such dedicated folk can only benefit the breed.

A quick mention to bring the figures on Obedience degrees more up to date.""Chips," the national Obedience magazine, reveals that in the four years from 1965 through 1968, 117 Norwegian Elkhounds received C.D. degrees, 13 achieved C.D.X., and 3 made U.D.

Laika III av Fjellbu. Bred by Bjorn Gronvold, Norway. Owned by Herb and Marie Stahl,

Ch. Tyr av Katrine Glen, with owner Henry M. Glasgow, Sr.

Ch. Norseman av Normandy. Bred by Norman L. Davis, Jr., and owned by Miss Margaret J. Kampish.

Left, Ch. Norseman av Normandy, bred by Norman L. Davis, Jr. Owned and handled by Kamgaard Kennels. Right, Norseman's son, Ch. Kamgaard Tryglikk Thor, bred, owned and handled by Kamgaard Kennels.

Ch. Crafdal Tryglik Trytta, C.D., owned by Bill Hoops.

Winning brace, Joywoods Jensine av Banik and Beata av Sangrad. Owner, Miss Miriam C. Phillips.

Ch. Binne av Norefjell with young owner, Candy Reiter.

Ar-Jo's Misty of Viewridge, owned by Mrs. Edward L. Koetje.

Ch. Silverstone Suri, owned by Silverstone Kennels.

Ch. Thuse of La Habra Hills. Bred by Luis and Etta M. Schleimer, and owned by Stuart L. and Janet K. Warter.

Ch. Ringo's Prince of La Habra Hills, owned by Dr. Sidney and Myrtle A. Rogers.

Can. Ch. Norsemen's Tor Rikke, bred, owned and handled by Mr. and Mrs. Harold Hobson.

Ch. Runefjell Borg av Norlys, bred by Mr. and Mrs. Lloyd Jackson, and owned by Dr. and Mrs. Malcolm B. Hanson.

Am. & Can. Ch. Norsemen's Satan Buster, bred and owned by Laura and Harold Hobson.

Am. & Can. Ch. Norsemen's Jens av Vikna.

Ch. Windy Cove Tass av Oftenasen, Norwegian import, Specialty Best in Show winner. Breeder, Magne Aftret. Owner, Mrs. Joe Peterson.

Ch. Windy Cove Golly Balmy Bee, owned by Dr. F. Audley Hale and Mrs. Joe Peterson.

Ch. Bjorn-Lass Niki, bred and owned by Bjorn-Lass Kennels.

Ch. Bjorn-Lass Torq, bred and owned by Bjorn-Lass Kennels.

Ch. Shawns Tory Fran Van, bred and owned by Mrs. Louis Franciose and Mrs. Charles Van Fleet.

Ch. Trygve of Keyport, bred by Mrs. Halvord Hoff, Keyport Kennels.

Ch. Wandec's Viceroy av Vin Melca, bred by Vin-Melca Kennels.

Ch. Silver Son's Danny av Vel-J-Nic, owned by W. N. Nichols.

Ch. Brawnko av Sorvestgaard at 16 mos. Owned by Ralph and Vichette A. Jones.

Am. & Can. Ch. So Merri Lady Wunderbar, bred by Beatrice A. Hall. Shown to both titles by owner-handler, 17-year-old Ed Hall.

August of Vine Hill, bred by Mary O. Jenkins, and owned by Mr. and Mrs. James Tichner.

So Merri Furstin Valentina, bred by Edward W. Hall, and owned by J. Herbert Hall.

Ch. Highland Branstock Renegade, Group winner. Owners, Dr. and Mrs. Jack Lewis.

Ch. Tryg av Valhall, owned by Daniel P. Haggerty.

Astrid av Vine Hill, bred by Vine Hill Kennels.

Ch. Sorvestgaard Kuuda, bred and owned by Ralph and Violette Jones.

Ch. Ericsgaard Fram, bred and owned by Sue Ann Erickson.

Ch. Savdajaura's Thor, owned by Mrs. Janet P. Kaplan.

Ch. Silver's Buck of Highland, bred by Highland Kennels.

Ch. Silver's Monty of Highland, top NEANC Phillips points winner for 1965. Owned by Gladys and Guy Cutter.

Ch. Aija's Fjell of Elkins, bred by Doris H. Phillips.

Ch. Aija's Kearsarge of Elkins, bred by Doris H. Phillips.

Ch. Mikkel of Keyport II, Hound Group winner. Owners, Dr. and Mrs. Robert A. Indeglia.

Ch. Black Bart av Boston, owned by James V. and Maxine Boston.

Friochan Ailsa, C.C. winner, bred and owned by Mrs. K. C. Heffer, England.

Ch. Woden, bred and owned by Mrs. George Powell, England.

Eng. Ch. Gerda of Eskamere.

7

Norwegian Elkhounds
in England

THE first Norwegian Elkhound registered in the *Kennel Club Stud Book* was Foerdig, 7848, whelped 1874, owned by Major Godfrey Faussett, breeder and pedigree unknown. From time to time a variety of specimens were brought over to England from Norway by sportsmen on fishing trips and the first imports were recorded in 1878. Three years later, Ch. Admiral, 11056, was imported by W. K. Taunton, who, in *The Illustrated Book of the Dog*, had this to say about his dog:

"My own dog Admiral was black mixed with gray, with white chest, legs and feet. I consider him the finest specimen I have seen; he was obtained for me direct from Norway by a friend who took considerable trouble to secure the best he could obtain. He was exhibited at the last Alexandra Palace show, where he was awarded a silver medal. He is an active, good-tempered dog and very companionable; and the breed only wants to be introduced into this country, when I think it would very quickly become a favorite with the public."

In those early days the Elkhound was variously known in England as Norrlandsk Spets, Grahund, Jamthund, Graa Dyrehund, Norwegian Bear Dog, and Norwegian Elk Dog. For many years the breed was shown in the Foreign Dog Class, where it sometimes competed with such breeds as Dogue de Bordeaux, Siberian Sled

Dog, and Esquimaux. Evidently there was considerable variation in color, some being dark gray, others black, light and tan, a few blue gray, and one sable and white. The Iceland Elkhound, Frigga, 1982B, was white.

Among the early Elkhounds registered with pedigree unknown were Kvik, Saleer, Leyswood Wolf, Thor II, and L'Homme de Niege. The last-named dog came from Lapland; Scandinavian King was imported from Sweden. Hon. W. Harbord's Sharpe mated to Blue produced Norse, Blue Bell, and Viking; while W. C. Atherton's Thelma mated to Blue produced Olga, Freda, Dr. Nansen, Wolf IV, and Flink. Leonard W. Beddowe had an imported bitch called Ingered, the dam of Fiord and Lapland Lassie. Dogs such as these and their offspring represented the breed in England prior to 1900.

The larger shows, such as Crystal Palace, had a few Elkhound entries, sufficient to provide bench show interest. About this time Jaeger more or less set the style for the breed as he was considered by the judges to be the most typical Elkhound. He was imported by Lady Cathcart from Swedish Lapland, where Sir Reginald Cathcart frequently hunted elk and bear with native dogs. Then as now, the Norwegians were loath to part with their best hunting dogs and asked enormous prices for them. Carthcart said that the best specimens were dark gray with straight legs, cat feet, dense rain-resistant coats, prick ears, fox-like faces, and double curled tails. Although the dogs seemed wild by nature when hunting, they were faithful and devoted to their owners.

Jaeger, 1986B (Pil ex Polka), whelped 1896, bred by S. Hanson, was dark gray, twenty inches high, and fifty pounds in weight. He was the fountainhead of the old English strains of Elkhound through his descendants such as Ch. King, Namsos, Clinker, Wolfram, Ch. Woden, Gerda, Ch. Thorvah, and Ch. Beltsa. Ch. King, 2221D (Jaeger ex Blue Bell), whelped April 11, 1898, bred by Rev. G. M. D. Longinotto, and owned by Major A. W. Hicks-Beach, won many prizes at shows.

Ch. Woden, 559AA (Wolfram ex Thelma), whelped in 1915, was bred and owned by Mrs. George Powell. This dog, considered one of the best of his time, was nicely balanced, medium sized, good headed with brown eyes, and had correct tail carriage. His nephew Jansen, a bigger dog with yellow eyes, was his frequent competitor in bench shows. From Woden and Feiga came Ch. Beltsa, Ch. Thorvah, Astrid, and Thor, who figure in the pedigrees of many present day champions. In fact, Astrid was the granddam of Ch. Markel of the Hollow.

Between 1900 and 1918, the breed faded to less than fifty registrations for the period. But after the war interest revived and in 1923 the British Elkhound Society was formed with Lady Dorothy Wood (Viscountess of Halifax) as President and Colonel G. J. Scovell as Secretary. On a visit to Norway the latter purchased some Glitre dogs from Veterinary Surgeon T. Hemsen (of Ski), Ch. Rugg av Glitre and Bjonn av Glitre. Bob and Binna av Glitre, both sired by Dyre av Glitre, also were imported, as well as Nora av Glitre and W. F. Holmes' Ch. Gaupa av Glitre. The last-named bitch, often referred to as the matriarch of the breed, was never defeated in British shows. These Glitre dogs, which were quite different from the old English dogs, influenced the breed greatly in Britain, and even in America, for many of their offspring went to the United States. W. F. Holmes' Ch. Rugg av Glitre won twenty-one certificates in England, Bob won fifteen, and Int. Ch. Peik II av Glitre won thirteen. The Norwegian dog Dyre av Glitre, who won twenty-seven certificates, sired such famous ones as Ch. Skrub, Rugg, Stryx, and Heika, all "av Glitre."

Ch. Wythall, who died at four years of age, was Rugg's most famous son; Ch. Brenda of Pannal (nine challenge certificates) was an outstanding daughter. From imported Ch. Finnegutten and Ch. Gaupa av Glitre came Ch. Patsy of the Holm, later exported to America. Ch. Garrowby Haakon, Gaupa's grandson, should be given great credit as a producer. It is reported that Gaupa inclined toward coarseness. A distinct outcross to the Glitre blood which came from Norway was the line from Sweden through Rulle, Ch. Lalla, and Ch. Carros. G. H. Harland's Ch. Kit and the Dogsthorpe dogs of W. Stuart-Thompson trace back to these Swedish strains. The imported Ch. Finnegutten, a son of Ch. Tas av Lifjell, was the first Elkhound to place in the Variety Group in England (1928).

In this era of importation there was great variation in type, but there gradually evolved from the medley the English stamp of Elkhound. Certainly the infusion of Norwegian and of Swedish blood contributed to improvement in bone and conformation. W. Stuart-Thompson said, "There is not a single Elkhound in England that

117

does not descend from Senny II or from Gerda, sister to Ch. Woden, even though these two brood matrons stem from two different Elkhound strains. They transmitted the correct type that they inherited."

Some of the prominent owners of Elkhounds prior to 1940 were: Commander R. F. Eyre, Mrs. A. Evans, Lt. Col. P. L. Reid, Mrs. F. C. Freeman-Taylor, S. Rogerson, Lady Violet Henderson, Mrs. L. Alford, Mrs. George Powell, W. Stuart-Thompson, J. G. Prentice, Mrs. M. Pryce, Mrs. E. E. Wilson, C. Mocatta, Lady Kitty Ritson, Mrs. G. M. Soame, Mrs. A. O. Lombe, Mrs. M. B. Benyon, Mrs. H. M. Fowler, Mrs. K. C. Heffer, Mrs. Bailey-Hamilton, G. H. Harland, Lady Dorothy Wood, and others.

One of the largest kennels of Elkhounds in England is Fourwents, owned by Mrs. Winter, formerly Miss F. Joyce Esdaile, Holmwood, Surrey. In the decade following 1929, she had six champion bitches: Int. Ch. Fourwents Brighde, Ch. Fourwents Fenya, Ch. Fourwents Sonja, Ch. Fourwents Grisla, Ch. Fourwents Minna, and American Ch. Fourwents Binne. There were five champion dogs: Int. Ch. Fourwents Gustav, Ch. Fourwents Dyfrin, Ch. Fourwents Frodi, Int. Ch. Fourwents Bring, and American Ch. Fourwents Paal. In 1938, Miss Esdaile became Secretary of the newly formed Elkhound Club. Shortly before World War II, she imported Ch. Varg av Skromte-fjell. Later Fourwents dogs of note include Ch. Fourwents Grinta, Fourwents Gota, Wota of the Holm, Fourwents Garbo, and Four-wents Froyen.

The world famous affix "of the Holm," which has been prominent for the last quarter of a century, belongs to W. F. Holmes, Hampton Wick. Among his dogs were Elsa of the Holm, Karl of the Holm, Kula of the Holm, Rosa of the Holm, Ch. Gaupa av Glitre, Ulla of the Holm, Fram of the Holm, Ula, Xeno of the Holm, Ch. Stryx av Glitre, Int. Ch. Peik II av Glitre, Ch. Rugg av Glitre, Ch. Krans av Glitre, Ch. Dick of the Holm, and Ch. Delia of the Holm. Mr. Holmes bred litters by the famous Ch. Garrowby Haakon and by Ch. Krans. He was President of the Elkhound Club, and through the years he has imported many dogs and also exported quite a few. In fact, most American Elkhounds have some "of the Holm" blood-lines. Ch. Patsy of the Holm, Ch. Marko of the Holm, and Ch. Greta of the Holm were among those dogs that were exported to America.

Eng. Ch. Dauna of Eskamere.

Eng. Ch. Touvere Thea.

Eng. Ch. Ardenwood Gunther.

Eng. Ch. Sian of Deri Ormond.

Another well-known affix is "of the Hollow," used by Mrs. L. F. G. Powys-Lybbe for the past twenty-five years. Famous dogs bearing this name include Ch. Martin of the Hollow, Ch. Mirkel of the Hollow, Ch. Marta of the Hollow, Ch. Anna of the Hollow, Ch. Lisken of the Hollow, Ch. Tora of the Hollow, Ch. Kren of the Hollow, Ch. Bodil of the Hollow, Ch. Gylfi of the Hollow, Signe of the Hollow, Shian of the Hollow and others. Kren, Gylfi, and Martin were brothers. Ch. Mirkel heads the list of producing sires tabulated by W. F. Holmes:

		Certificates
1.	Ch. Mirkel of the Hollow (England)	31
2.	Dyre av Glitre (Norway)	27
3.	Ch. Finnegutten (England)	22
4.	Ch. Rugg av Glitre (England)	21
5.	Bov av Glitre (England)	15
6.	Kvinsen (England)	15
7.	Int. Ch. Peik II av Glitre (England)	13
8.	Ch. Garrowby Haakon (England)	12
9.	Ch. Tass av Lifjell (Norway)	12
10.	Ch. Krans (England)	10
11.	Ch. Woden (England)	9
12.	Ch. Wythall (England)	9
13.	Wolfram (England)	8
14.	Ch. Martin of the Hollow (U.S.A.)	8
15.	Ch. Skrub av Glitre (Norway)	7

The Jarlsberg Kennels of Miss Gerd Berbom, a Norwegian girl who lived in England for a while and then in Norway, have been noted for Lasse av Hyna, Bamse av Jarlsberg, and Ch. Steig av Jarlsberg. Then there are the Garrowby Kennels of Viscountess Halifax; the Friochan Kennels of Mrs. K. C. Heffer; the Aalesund Kennels of Charles N. Thompson; and the Inverailort Kennels of Mrs. C. H. J. Cameron-Head.

The pattern of Elkhound breeding in England changed considerably after the Second World War. Many of the pre-war kennels had been dispersed and their owners did not recommence breeding. Newcomers to the breed were unable to run large establishments due to difficulties in finding staff, and of course, for the first few years, problems of feeding. However, they carried on as best they could with fewer dogs and coping by themselves without any help.

The first post-war champion was Bamse av Jarlsberg, brought from Norway in 1946 by Miss Gerd Berbom. Bamse sired many winners and was used at stud extensively in the breed before returning to Norway with his owner. Other imports from Norway were Mrs. Powys Lybbe's Gaupestein Ruggen in 1947, Mrs. Heffer's Glennas Rugg in 1948, and—several years later—Mrs. Kincaid-Lennox's Tortasen's Moman.

The "of the Holm" Kennels owned by Mr. W. F. Holmes, have been known world-wide since 1924, and they are still the largest kennel of the breed in England today, standing in eight acres of ground with very large runs and ideal conditions for rearing Elkhounds. Ch. Yama and Ch. Yacca of the Holm, two litter sisters, were Mrs. Powys-Lybbe's Gaupestein Ruggen in 1947, Mrs. Heffer's Ch. Narvik of the Holm, ancestor of most of the winning Holms today. Ch. Essen of the Holm was sired by Mrs. Kincaid-Lennox's Norwegian import, Tortasen's Moman. Other more recent champions are Ch. Musti and Ch. Lapp of the Holm.

The Fourwents Kennels of Mrs. Winter (formerly Miss F. J. Esdaile) were active immediately after the War. The first champion was Fourwents Rugg av Aalesund, winner of many Challenge Certificates and sire of numerous good progeny before going to America, where he quickly added his American championship. Another well-known champion was the bitch, Fourwents Trigg. After her marriage, Mrs. Winter was unable to continue with her kennels, but has just recently returned to the show ring and made up Ch. Fourwents Gretel of Eskamere. Also from Fourwents' blood came the famous English and Irish Ch. Lofoten Anton, owned and bred by Mr. and Mrs. Iorns. Anton was the winner of 18 Certificates, and the sire of Ch. Ravenstone Humourist and Ch. Henningsvaer Lief. He died several years ago.

The Friochan Kennels of Mrs. K. C. Heffer are also very well-known, both pre-war and up to the present day, and Mrs. Heffer is a keen and active member of the Elkhound world. The Norwegian import, Ch. Glennas Rugg, was her first post-war champion, and he was used on many different bloodlines, producing a great number of successful winning progeny including his son, Ch. Friochan Dolf. Other Friochan champions are Friochan Valda, Friochan Alvar and Friochan Horsa.

The Touvere Kennel, owned by Mrs. A. G. Harris, started in 1948. Ch. Timba of Coddington, bred by the late Mrs. Hunt, was the founder of the Touveres. From several matings with Anna of Ewerne he sired Ch. Touvere Viva, Ch. Touvere Thane, Ch. Count Oluf and the well-known bitch, Ch. Touvere Thea, winner of 22 Challenge Certificates. He was also the sire of Ch. Friochan Valda and Ch. Jotsoma Buster. Other Touvere champions were Touvere Kren, Touvere Frieda, Touvere Norsk, Touvere Rolf, Touvere Sturla, and Touvere Gerda.

The Ravenstone Kennels of Miss A. M. Lovell have produced many champions and winning Elkhounds in recent years. The foundation bitch of this kennel was Ch. Ravenstone Falda of Ardenwood, bred by Miss Legg. Falda was the dam of four champions, three by Ch. Gunnar of Coddington (Ch. Ravenstone Crim and the litter brothers, Ch. Ravenstone Gunnar and American Ch. Ravenstone Gunstig), and one by Ch. Lofoten Anton (the bitch, Ch. Ravenstone Humourist). Her most famous son was Ch. Ravenstone Gunnar, who proved himself to be a prepotent sire, producing eleven English champions, two American champions, and many other quality first-prize winners from a variety of bloodlines.

The small but successful Eskamere Kennel was started in 1961 by Mrs. A. Heward. In the first litter, by Ch. Ravenstone Gunnar out of Toelsuba Gerda, were bred the litter sisters Chs. Solveig and Karen of Eskamere. Toelsuba Gerda, who won two Challenge Certificates, unfortunately died of a virus infection. However, her daughter Solveig also produced two champions in her first litter, Ch. Gerda of Eskamere and Ch. Fourwents Gretel of Eskamere. The other daughter, Ch. Karen of Eskamere, owned by Mrs. Millis, was the dam of Ch. Dauna of Eskamere, owned by Mr. and Mrs. Poole.

The late Ch. Sian of Deri Ormond, owned by Mrs. T. Thomas, was one of the most famous bitches of post-war years, being the

Eng. & Irish Ch. Lofoten Anton.

Eng. Ch. Ravenstone Gunnar
(at 6 yrs.)

Eng. Ch. Ravenstone Kell.

winner of 23 Challenge Certificates, several Bests in Show at Championship shows, and—in 1957—Best Hound and Best in Show the first day at Crufts. This is a record unequalled by any other Elkhound dog or bitch. She was the dam of Ch. Ardenwood Zeeta of Deri Ormond.

The following-named kennels, with their owners identified in parentheses, have also been well-known in the breed in post-war years: Greydale (Mr. G. Harland); Kinburn (Mrs. Kincaid-Lennox); Whiteway (Mrs. de la Poer Beresford); Lofoten (Mr. and Mrs. W. Iorns); Thingvollr (Mrs. M. Hutchinson); Torden (Mrs. Harburn); Karworth (Mr. L. P. Wadsworth); Deri Ormond (Mrs. T. Thomas); Ardenwood (Miss E. Legg); Jotsoma (Mr. W. Carey); Trulsmoi (Mr. R. M. Kennett); Kistrand (Miss E. Wilson); Lillabo (Miss E. M. Langman); Mindas (Mrs. M. Parkes); Elkholme (Mrs. M. Basher); and Tortawe (Mr. and Mrs. D. H. Griffiths).

There are usually forty or more Elkhounds entered at most Championship Shows, so the competition is keen. There are two breed clubs in England—the British Elkhound Society and the Elkhound Club, and in Scotland there is the Elkhound Association of Scotland.

Can. Ch. Norsemen's Tor Rikke, at 8 weeks of age.

8

Norwegian Elkhounds in Holland

by Dr. H. Bonnema, Netherlands
(from *Om Elghunder og Eljakt i Norge de Siste 50 Ar.*)

AS far back as I can remember, I have always lived in the company of dogs. I, myself, cannot remember the following episode, but my mother has often told of the humorous happening.

When I was a baby, about six or seven months old, my mother went to visit with some of her friends. My father served as baby-sitter for his first born. It so happened that my mother did not get home in due time, and I got very hungry. Like other children in this circumstance, I began to cry. My father was at a loss as to what to do for his very hungry offspring. But then he had an inspiration. Our English Setter, "Labora," was nursing a litter of six puppies, and so my father reasoned that what was good for the puppies should be good for the baby. It certainly worked out fine. When my mother came home she found me lying between the puppies, well-fed and sound asleep.

The first dog that I can remember was a Scotch sheepdog. He was born on my birthday, and of course he was my dog. His name was Mack, and he was with me in swimming and in play. He slept in front of my bed every night, and we were the best of friends for all those many years.

As long as I was home with my folks it was easy to keep one or more dogs. But when I grew up and went to the University, having a dog in a small rented room became a problem. It seemed I was always on the move because of complaints: "Your dog is barking," "He has chewed a chair leg to pieces," etc. But nevertheless, I kept my dog during my school years.

After finishing my education, I was married. Alas, my wife did not like dogs—she was scared of them. As a wedding present, I gave her a Griffon named Nimmie. He was sweet and funny, and it was not long before they were great friends.

When the Germans invaded Holland, they ran over Nimmie. He died, but he had done his bit—my wife had learned to love dogs.

As a doctor with a wide and busy practise in my district, I had very little chance to raise dogs. But following the occupation, I had more leisure time. It was then that in looking through some hunting magazines, I found a picture of a Norwegian Elghund. It was love at first sight. I showed the picture to my wife, and she agreed that the Elghund was the dog for the future.

There were no Norwegian Elghunds in Holland at that time, and Norway was a long way off. I knew no one in that country who could give me information on the dogs. Happily, it was not so far over to England, and in that country they also had Elghunds. I had some good friends there who could help me with advice.

After much correspondence with my friends in England, I purchased Fourwents Vida, a 7-month-old bitch by Varg av Alvdal ex Fourwents Kora, and Fourwents Bjorg, a 4-months-old male by Bamse av Jarlsberg ex Dox Nitra. Vida came quickly by air, and Bjorg came 14 days later.

At the time, they were the only two Elghunds in Holland. They were handsome, friendly, and had very nice personalities. Their first winter in our country was a cold one with quite a bit of snow, and so they had lots of fun.

From Sweden, I imported two of Miss Netta Duyvendak's Elghunds, but both died of distemper.

Vida's first litter presented us with ten puppies, the first Elghunds born in Holland. Of that litter, two were males—Arne and Annar. Ten puppies may have been too much for one dog, but Vida was healthy and all of the puppies looked good. I did not have the heart to destroy any of them. Through the first week all went well. But on the ninth day, when I came home Vida did not come out to greet me. I called, and she finally came out with stiff paws. She had developed purpural fever, and died the same evening. Then, I thought, I have not only lost Vida, but I will also lose the puppies.

My wife started to call all the dog breeders, and finally located a Great Dane that had three puppies 5-weeks old. Thus it happened that the first Elghund puppies born in Holland grew up on Great Dane milk.

When I asked the Raad van Beheer (the Holland equivalent of the American Kennel Club) if they could recommend a judge for the Norwegian Elghunds, they informed me that there was no judge in Holland at that time who knew anything about the Elghunds. So the Raad van Beheer appointed a Shepherd judge to pass upon the Elghunds. When we came to the dog show where he was judging, he looked at our dogs, and said "M-m-m, so these are Elghunds."

Obviously we could not depend upon these judges for expert decision. My wife and I decided to learn the Norwegian language, and then to take a trip to Norway to see and learn as much as possible about the breed. In Norway, we were made very welcome by Mr. Sven Mjearum, secretary of the Norsk Elghund Club. We visited many kennels, and had the opportunity of seeing Trysil-Knut, a handsome dog that belongs to Mr. Karl Opset. My wife purchased a son of Trysil-Knut. We joined the Norsk Kennel Club and received the magazine Hunde-Sport. Sometime later I imported a young female, Jossa av Skromtefjell, from Sven Mjearum's Skrom-tefjell Kennels in Norway.

Since 1949 many Elghunds have been imported in Holland from Norway, England, and the United States. We have also started an Elghund Club, and have had Norwegian judges here for some of our large Elghund shows.

One of the foremost pioneers in Norwegian Elkhound breeding in Holland is a lady that is no stranger to the American Elkhound fancy. She is Baroness Susan Van Boetzelaer, owner of the Riverland Kennels. The niece of Lawrence Litchfield, one of the founders of the Norwegian Elkhound Association of America, she has judged Elkhounds in the United States on several occasions, placing the dogs shown under her with great knowledge of the purpose and function of the breed.

Her original Elkhound, acquired from Litchfields, was Lulu of Lindvangen (Ch. Thormin of Gray Dawn ex Ch. Helga of Lindvangen). Lulu became one of the foundation dogs of the breed in Holland as the Baroness and several other dedicated breeders imported stock from England, Sweden and Norway. Combining the bloodlines of Lindvangen, Tallo, and the Hollow, Dutch breeders have attempted to preserve the hunting qualities and ideal breed temperament. Their breedings have produced such outstanding dogs as Ch. Martini of Riverland, Ch. Bimbi, and Skol van de Waddenkust.

Several Riverland dogs have been imported to North America from Holland. The W. R. Torrances of Winnipeg, Canada have received the bitch Ondine of Riverland from the Baroness, and she has figured prominently in their breeding program.

On an extended tour of the United States in 1965, Baroness Van Boetzelaer showed the dog that accompanied her, Odin of Riverland. He won consistently against American competition until his untimely death. The Baroness and the Riverland dogs provide a substantial link of good-will between Holland and North America.

Canadian Norwegian Elkhounds, Boetzke of Riverland (bitch) with Torr's Grayling (male).

9

Norwegian Elkhounds in Canada

No country in the world has greater potential for being the ideal realm of the Norwegian Elkhound than has our neighbor to the North. Canada has the endless wilderness, the deep woods, and the wide forests. It is a land tremendously rich in large and small game, with thousands of moose. elk deer and caribou, along with such marauders as wolves, mountain lions and coyotes. It is a hunter's paradise, a land rich in untapped natural resources, but it must be controlled and protected.

The Elkhound is quite new to Canada. The kennels are few and far between, so it may yet be possible to promote this excellent breed as a big game hunter, and in time it could reach the high level of such recognition that it enjoys in the Scandinavian countries.

If Elkhound breeders and owners are interested in helping to save the breed, and its reputation as a big game hunter and tracker, they must act soon. A strong league must be formed for protection and promotion of the Norwegian Elkhound, and the majority of members should be hunters, field-trial-interested men and women, and some outstanding sports writers. Their first objective should be to proclaim a slogan such as "Don't Make a Sissy of the Norwegian Elkhound!"

The next thing would be to change his name to Elghund (not Elkhound), which would help to clarify some of the confusion that now exists. The league would need a man who could work with the newspapers, magazines, and of course, with the Canadian National Live Stock, and with the Natural Resources Commission. I am sure they would get great help from Norway's Elghunters. They would bring over some of the best hunting dogs, and show the Canadian hunters and Conservation Department the sensible way to harvest the big game.

Let us hope that the Elkhound in Canada will become the famous dog of the country, and that in the future he will be well guarded and protected by a strong and tough association that "talks softly, but carries a big stick." The breeders must be kept in line, not with force but with a deep understanding of this breed's saga and its great future.

One of the pioneer kennels for Norwegian Elkhounds in Canada has been the Vakker-Lund Kennels, owned by Mr. and Mrs. John Terrely, of Gravenhurst, Ontario. They have produced not only fine show dogs, but also dogs that are good moose, deer and bear hunters.

Some years ago one of their dogs, on a moose hunt, got lost. The Terrelys spent 40 days in the wilderness in search of the dog. The dog was found, and returned to the Terrelys on Christmas evening, strong and healthy. What a Christmas that must have been!

It just goes to show what the Elkhound is made of; he can live off the land if he has to, and still look good in the show ring. That is a combination that is hard to beat.

The Terellys have shown their Elkhounds all over Canada, and at many shows in the United States. Ch. Vakker-Lund Buster is the most famous of the many handsome Elkhounds of their kennels. The show champion and the moose-hunting Elkhound should be one and the same. If we had more of the Vakker-Lund type of kennels in North America, the Elkhound would be on a solid foundation.

Mr. and Mrs. W. R. Torrance, owners of the Torr Kennels in Headingley, Manitoba, purchased their first Elkhound in 1955 and he became their first champion—Ch. Bairnley's Life of Norfin, C.D. Since then they have become avid students of the breed.

From Baroness Van Boetzelaer of Holland they purchased Guy

Can. Ch. Yokipi Vala av Halv Aker, owned by Mr. and Mrs. Spence.

Can. Ch. Torr's Prince Peter, C.D., owned by Marra Stein.

Can. Ch. Coulee Meadows Kip, owned by Mr. and Mrs. Spence.

Can. Ch. Tall Grass Kara, owned by Mr. and Mrs. Karl S. Innes.

Fawkes of Riverland, a very handsome dog that has many Bests of Breed and some Group placings. He has both his bench championship and a C.D.X. Obedience title. (Mrs. Torrance has taught Obedience for eight years, and has been the Obedience representative from Manitoba to the Canadian Kennel Club for three years.) Although they have many acres to use for runs, the Torrances breed on a very limited scale, preferring to have few, but all good ones.

The Karin Kennels of Mrs. Barbara A. Innes, Oshawa, Ontario, has bred dogs for years and has had many breeds. Finally, they started to breed Elkhounds, and that was it. From then on, it was Norwegian Elkhounds, and only Norwegian Elkhounds.

Their first female was Ch. Tall Grass Kara. In 1964, Karin enjoyed back-to-back thrills in seeing a puppy win Best of Breed and Best Canadian Puppy in Show one day, and then having his brother repeat with the same honors on the next day. There are now five fine Elkhounds in the kennel.

When Mr. and Mrs. Arulf Flaten of Cumberland, Ontario, decided to raise Norwegian Elkhounds, it was no fooling around with these folk. From Norway they imported the now Can. Ch. Storm, bred by Ingebridt, Lodoen, Norway, and of Suteraas bloodline. J. Hallingby of Norway selected Sonja av Suteraas for them, bred by Christian and Oskar Svae of Norway. Sonja also has some Suteraas blood, as well as Kotofjell. Now the Flatens are looking forward to the first litter of these imports.

Mr. and Mrs. H. O. Swanson of Ottawa, Ontario, acquired their first Elkhound back in 1954. She was Margot of Greenwood, the daughter of Ch. Lady Kazana of Greenwood. Mr. Swanson was then in the Foreign Service of the United States Government, and Margot went wherever the Swansons did, adjusting herself very well to the change of climate and different homes. In 1966, the Swansons established their Valgtor Kennels. They are the owners of Ch. Norsemen's Unnlepe Kunstner, a handsome dog that has won lots of prizes in Canada, and of a promising young female, Can. Ch. Norsemen's Mi Nydelig Valg.

First Elkhound for Mr. and Mrs. James Spence, of the Yokipi Kennels in Richmond, B.C., was Yogi, an excellent Obedience training dog that scored 199 points in her first competition. With the purchase of Coulee Meadows Kip (from Mr. and Mrs. Pugh of Ephrata, Washington) and of Vala, a female, the Spences are

Can. Ch. Torr's Silver Drey of Shonleh, C.D., owned by Sharon Curry and Dawn Fee.

Can. Ch. Norsemen's Valgtor Skjelmsk, owned by Mrs. Alice S. Swanson.

Karin's Breckin, bred by Mr. and Mrs. Karl Innes, and owned by E. R. Norum of Saskatchewan.

Can. Ch. Storm, owned by Mr. and Mrs. Arnulf Flaten.

launched in the breeding of Norwegian Elkhounds. To their mind, there is no finer breed than the National Dog of Norway.

It is heartwarming to find some young folks who are so interested in the Norwegian Elkhound that they take the time to write on different aspects of the breed—hunting and hunting-type Elkhounds, the standard, and training the Elkhound. One such person is Marra Stein, Tuxedo, Manitoba. Her dog is Ch. Prince Peter, bred by Torr Kennels. In one show, Peter made something of a record—finishing his championship in conformation, and then completing his C.D. in Obedience, all within a half hour!

Ch. Borgny av Runefjell, owned by Luther Tollesfrud.

Walter Moore with Wabeth dog sled team. Wabeth Toralf of Greenwood is the lead dog.

Melvin Lightle of Auburn, Wash. on a Canadian trap line.

135

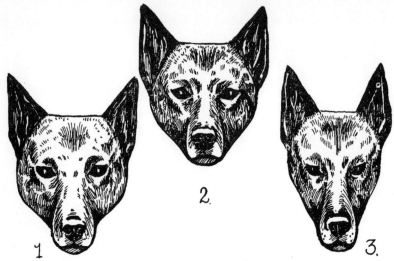

1. Wide skull—pinched foreface
2. Correct—wedge shaped
3. Narrow—fox-like

1. Narrow and wrinkled between close set ears
2. Too much stop—too much ruff—low set ears
3. Correct side view of head

10

Official Breed Standard of the Norwegian Elkhound

Submitted by the Norwegian Elkhound Club of America, and approved by the American Kennel Club, July, 1969.

General Description—The Norwegian Elkhound is a typical Northern dog, of medium size, with a compact, proportionately short body, with a thick and rich, but not bristling, gray coat, with prick ears, and with a tail that is curled and carried over the back. His temperament is bold and energetic.

Head—"Dry" (without any loose skin), broad at the ears; the forehead and back of the head only slightly arched; the stop not large, yet clearly defined. The muzzle is of medium length, thickest at the base and, seen from above or from the side, tapers evenly without being pointed. The bridge of the nose is straight; the lips are tightly closed.

Ears—Set high, firm and erect, are higher than they are wide at the base, pointed (not rounded) and very mobile. When the dog is listening, the orifices are turned forward.

Eyes—Not protruding, brown in color, preferably dark, lively, with a fearless energetic expression.

Neck—Of medium length, "dry" (without any loose skin), strong, and well set up.

Body—Powerful, *compact,* and short, with broad deep chest, well-sprung ribs, straight back, well-developed loins, and stomach very little drawn-up.

Legs—Firm, straight and strong; elbows closely set on; hind legs with little angulation at knees and hocks. Seen from behind, they are straight.

Feet—Comparatively small, somewhat oblong, with tightly closed toes, not turned out. There should be no dewclaws on hind legs.

Tail—Set high, short, thickly and closely haired, but without brush; tightly curled, not carried too much to one side.

Coat—Thick, rich and hard, but rather smooth-lying. On head and front of legs, short and even; longest on neck and chest, on buttocks, on hindside of forelegs and on underside of tail. It is made up of longer and harder covering hairs, dark at the tips, and of a light, soft, woolly undercoat.

Color—Gray, with black tips to the long covering hairs; somewhat lighter on chest, stomach, legs, underside of tail, and around anus. The color may be lighter or darker, with a slight shading towards yellow; but a pronounced variation from the gray color disqualifies. Too dark or too light individuals should be avoided; also, yellow markings or uneven coloring. There should be no pronounced white markings.

Height at Shoulder—The ideal height for dogs, $20\frac{1}{2}$ inches; for bitches, $19\frac{1}{4}$ inches.

DISQUALIFICATION

Pronounced variation from gray color.

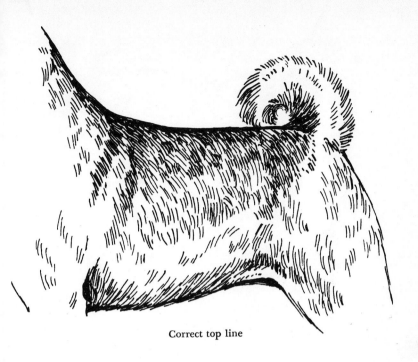

Correct top line

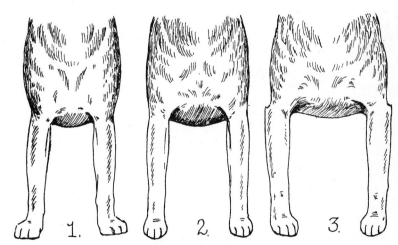

1. Narrow—pinched elbows—toes out
2. Correct—straight—toes forward
3. Too wide—elbows out—toes in

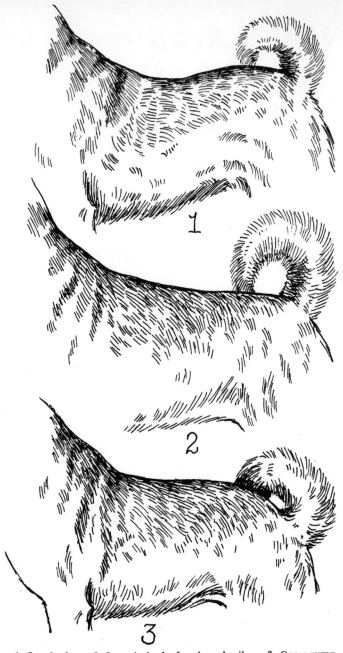

1. Swayback.   2. Long in back—fan-shaped tail.   3. Goose rump.

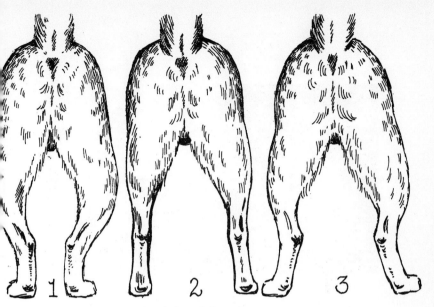

1. Bandy-legged (bowed)
2. Correct rear
3. Cowhocks

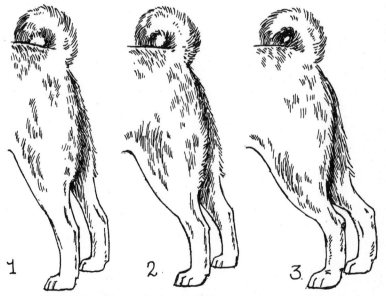

1. Straight stifles.   2. Correct side rear.   3. Over-angulation.

A handsome Crafdal trio—"Bamsi," "Loki," and immortal "Tryg."

11

An Elaboration upon the Standard

THE present standard of the Norwegian Elkhound, which is a translation of the Norwegian one, was adopted by the American Kennel Club in 1935, and revised (as to height) in 1969. Although the Standard is a definite specification, it seems advisable to interpret certain parts of it in detail in order to present a clear mental picture of the perfect Elkhound. One thing that should be emphasized at the start is that the Elkhound is a hunting breed that must possess the necessary physical qualifications to serve its purpose.

Personality—The Elkhound's personality is different from that of any other breed of dogs, no doubt as a result of his long and close association with mankind. He has an unusual attachment toward his owner and is most friendly, loyal, and dependable. He seems to like nothing better than to be an important member of the family—in fact, he enjoys being the center of attraction. Noted for his gentle disposition and even temperament, he seldom starts a fight with other dogs. Yet he is bold and aggressive and has plenty of nerve when facing big game. As a guardian of the home and other property, this Viking dog shows understanding and intelligence far beyond expectation.

General Appearance—He is a medium-sized, compact, rugged Northern dog with square outline; thick, gray, smooth-lying, not bristling coat; pointed, prick ears; and tightly curled tail carried over the back. There should be balance and harmony in his conformation, which will contribute both to his use and to his beauty.

Height—The ideal height at the withers for males is 20½ inches (52 cm.) and for females 19¼ inches (49 cm.). It is pointed out that the variation from these measurements should not exceed 1 inch.

Weight—Although weight is not specified in the Standard, it is usually considered to be approximately 55 to 60 pounds for dogs and 45 to 50 pounds for bitches. Elkhound size should be guarded carefully, because a big, clumsy dog is not suited for the natural work for which this breed was developed. Such a dog will tire too easily and his feet will become sore on rough terrain. He will lack the quickness and agility required of a big-game hunter; and on the trail of the moose, he will pull too hard in the harness. Elkhound size has evidently been well controlled, judging by a comparison of past and present day dogs. It is desirable to have size without coarseness.

Head—Very important is the head, for undoubtedly the first impression is created by it. A dog with a poor head, even though he be good otherwise, does not have universal appeal. The description of the Elkhound head by T. Hemsen in *Om Elghunder og Elgjakt i Norge de Siste 50 Ar* is well worth quoting:
"The head of the purebred Elkhound is rather large and very distinctive. It is the head that one first looks at to see if the dog is pure. Elkhound characteristics carry along for generations and when mixed with other breeds, they predominate. For example, a mixture of Elkhound and Shepherd will exhibit mostly Elkhound characteristics. The head, which is typically wedge-shaped, must not be too pinched, tight, or dry ahead of the eyes. Viewed from above, the line from nose to ear should be straight; and viewed from the side, the top lines of the skull and the nose should be parallel. The skull is a little higher than the muzzle. It is slightly rounded, but from the side fairly straight. Eyebrows define a little stop. Under

lines of the lips conform with the jaw and do not bend upward at the front. The snoot must be strong and of good size at the tip, so that it does not appear snipish, especially for males. The muzzle length for males of medium size is normally 9 cm. (3½ inches) ; for females 8 cm. (3⅛ inches) . The inside of the lips is dark slate color. The tongue is flesh color. A rounded skull, which is a big fault, seems to be more and more common recently. It makes the head not typical; the stop is too great and the side lines curve inward with a pinched muzzle ahead of the eyes. If we hope to eliminate the fault we must not breed dogs having that fault, nor award them prizes. The skin of the head shall be dry with no wrinkles."

Emphasis should be placed on a wide, full skull, which is one of the basic features of the breed. The bridge of the nose should be straight, not dish-faced or Roman-nosed. The muzzle terminates in nicely finished nostrils, which should be wide open, moist, and dark, but never flesh colored.

Stop—There should be a definite but slight stop. The medium line continues up one-third of the forehead between slightly raised brows.

Mouth—The mouth should be cut back 3 to 3½ inches. The lips, which should be of fairly thin leather, must not extend beyond the jaw; yet they should cover the teeth when the mouth is closed.

Whiskers—The whiskers, which are dark and of medium length, should not be cut or trimmed.

Teeth—Strong, white teeth are essential. A scissors bite is correct, in which the inner surfaces of the upper teeth engage part of the outer surfaces of the lower teeth. Very seldom does one find an overshot or an undershot mouth in Elkhounds.

Eyes—One of the most cherished characteristics of a dog is his eyes, for they determine the expression, which in the case of the Elkhound should be sparkling, frank, fearless, and friendly. They should be of medium size, dark brown, slightly almond shaped, not round or protruding, if anything rather deep-set, about two inches apart, not on the edges of the skull, with no haws showing, and with tight dark-rimmed lids. The iris fills the whole eye opening, so that the white of the eyeball does not show. At night the eyes are often a luminous green. Light eyes should be penalized.

Ears—The temperament of an Elkhound is reflected by his ears, which are very mobile and quick to respond to his feelings. The ears are open forward when the dog is alert or excited, are dropped when he is depressed or sick, and are laid back for affection or when he is in full run. Sometimes they are laid back right on the neck which might erroneously give the impression of a mean disposition. Although the ears should be vertical, one occasionally finds them pointing outward, which may be due to the fact that they are low set or that the dog is sluggish. Ears are usually erect in puppies at five to ten weeks of age. The Elkhound ear should be pointed, but not acute like that of a German Shepherd; its height should exceed the width at the base approximately by an inch; and as a rule, the size lies between that of a German Shepherd and that of an Alaskan Husky. The ear, which should open to the front, should be neither too fine nor too coarse in texture or substance. The set of the ears when erect should be fairly high on the skull with no wrinkles; they should be carried slightly forward and they should be wide apart but not on the corners of the skull so as to appear flat across like mule ears. The ear box is small. Hair on the ears is short and fine. There is hair in the outer ear to protect against dirt and other foreign material. It seems that the Elkhound has an exceptionally keen sense of hearing and as a breed is not prone to deafness with age.

Neck—A neck of medium length, muscular, flexible, arched, and not quite round is desirable. It should be dry and clean where it joins the head and taper smoothly but strongly into the shoulders. The skin is loose on the nape of the neck, but must be dry on the under side, i.e., without dewlap. A fat dog usually stores excess fat there. An important characteristic of the neck is the ruff or collar, which is the profuse, stand-off coat on the neck. The appearance of power is magnified by this collar. An upright neck, known in Norway as *good rising,* is much more stylish than one in horizontal line with the back.

Shoulders—It seems that *good rising* as well as the relative length of the neck, body, and stride, all are based on the length and slope of the shoulder blades. Short, upright blades are associated with a short neck, long back, and choppy steps. In contrast, long sloping shoulder blades accompany a long neck, short back, and smooth stride. Elkhound shoulders, however, are not as sloping as those of bird dogs. The blades should be of wide bone with good texture. They should be close together at the withers and well laid back. Loose shoulders are a bad fault. The muscles should be long, smooth, and strong rather than short and bulging.

Appropriate here are these observations made by Olav Roig, General Secretary of the Norsk Kennel Club, and one of the foremost experts on osteology:

> The conception of the function of a dog's shoulder blade (scapula) has undergone quite an evolution during the past sixty years.
>
> The function of the scapula was first described by the German cynologist, Captain Max v. Stephanitz, at the beginning of this century. Max v. Stephanitz believed that the scapula was firmly fixed to the rib cage of the dog, and launched his well-known theory of the 90% front leg angulation. Based on the assumption that the scapula did not move, von Stephanitz theorized that the optimum angle on the vertical line should be 45°. Accordingly, with the scapula and the humerus forming an angle of 90°, the greatest stride of the front leg should be achieved when all its joints were stretched to 180°. Thus, dogs whose front legs could make the longest stride were believed to have the most efficient gait.
>
> In the 1930's two major flaws in Max v. Stephanitz's theory were brought to the attention of dog fanciers. It was pointed out, as veterinarians have always known, that the scapula of the dog is *not* joined to the rib cage, nor is it at all connected with the rest of the skeleton as in man. It was shown that when the dog moves there is also a substantial movement of the scapula. It was further pointed out that if the von Stephanitz theory were true, the foot of the front leg would not touch the ground when the front leg was stretched forward.
>
> Although the von Stephanitz theory was proven false more than thirty years ago, this does not mean that all authors of popular dog books are aware of the fact.
>
> Since the 1930's it has been acknowledged that the movement of the front leg takes place mainly in the shoulder region as the scapula hinges on the central muscle area, and that the movement of joints of the front legs merely supplement the movement of the scapula.

With the era of ultra slow-motion film it was discovered that in addition to the movement of the scapula hinged on the central muscle area, the scapula also moves backward and forward along the rib cage. As the front leg is stretched forward and the foot reaches the ground, the scapula lies well forward on the rib cage. Then the dog literally hauls its body forward with the aid of its shoulder muscles. The scapula is then in a position considerably further back at the end of the stride of the front leg.

Detailed studies have proved that the distance that the scapula moves varies substantially from one dog to another within the same breed. However, dogs with a very efficient gait show the forward and backward movement of the scapula so clearly that, provided the observer is aware of what to look for, it may be observed with the naked eye under normal conditions.

Body—The body should be compact, square, and short; but not so short that it is rigid and stiff.

Chest—A broad, and at the same time deep, chest is desirable. For a medium-sized dog the width should be 9 to 10 inches. The chest should not be so wide, however, that it causes a waddling gait. Neither should it be shallow or barrel-round. The girth of chest of a mature Elkhound in good condition may be 29 to 31 inches. When viewed from the front, the shoulders appear somewhat flat and the brisket appears oval and keel-shaped, but not narrowed to a point. The breastbone should carry well through between the forearms to contribute to a pleasing front line from the chin to the toes when viewed in profile.

Ribs—The body should be well ribbed to furnish sufficient space for the lungs, heart, and other vital organs. The curvature of the chest box is heartform in cross section. The rib bones themselves are flat and the back ones must be of good length.

Loin—One of the most important specifications of the breed is that the loin should be short. Two and a half inches is a very short loin. There should be little tuck-up; in other words, the loin should be deep as well as wide, and very slightly arched.

Top Line—The back should be short and strong with *good rising* and a gradual slope from the withers down to the tail. The difference in height at the withers and at the hips is usually less than one inch.

Under Line—Seen in profile the under line is nearly horizontal. There is a fairly deep flank.

Hips—The hips should be wide, muscular, and but slightly sloping to the root of the tail. A goose rump is a bad fault.

Forelegs—The forelegs, which should be straight, sturdy, and of good bone, should be flat rather than round. The forearms should be short, most of the dog's height being attained from the elbow upward to the withers. Forelegs are set back at the elbows, which should be directly under the top points of the shoulder blades, i.e., definitely not "Terrier-fronted." Elbows should not be pinched as is often the case with dogs that toe out. This cramps the chest. On the other hand, a dog out at the elbows usually toes in, possesses excessive width of chest, and moves with a waddling gait (not in a straight line) .

Both elbow and knee joints, as well as hocks, should be broad and strong. The tendons attached to them should extend over considerable length for efficient leverage. Front pasterns, which should be short and of good substance, should be very nearly upright. Too straight pasterns are likely to knuckle over in sudden stops or quick turns, as down hill in rugged country; whereas too sloping pasterns are weak.

T. Hemsen says, "The legs must not be too thin, but in a natural way they must harmonize with the dog's structure. The front legs should stand a good distance apart viewed from the front, and must be straight from the shoulder to the ground, for the elbows must not be loose or pinched. From the side, the front legs must also be straight with little bending in the pasterns."

Hind Legs—"The rear legs must also stand well apart when viewed from behind and must be parallel. If they are too close together, it is because the pelvis is too narrow or the stance is crooked. From the side the rear legs should have a little but distinct angulation in hocks and knee, in order that the dog can react with lightning movement. The lower leg must always stand approximately vertical, but not farther back than the root of the tail."

In general, the hind legs must be muscular, wide and thick with little angulation in stifle (knee) and hock. Too straight stifles produce a stilted action. The distance from hock to foot can be too short as well as excessively long; its proportion should be pleasing, and efficient mechanically for the work that is to be done. There shall be no dewclaws on the hind legs.

Feet—Elkhound feet must be comparatively small, somewhat oblong, compact, and with thick, tough pads. They are not cat feet; neither are they hare feet. The toes, which should point forward and be close together, should be well arched with protective hair between them. Open, splayed feet with thin pads have a tendency to ball up with ice in thawing winter weather. They will not stand the rough going in rugged country. The nails, which should be dark gray and of medium length, should touch the ground when the dog is standing normally. Furthermore, they should be very strong to grip the ground when the dog is in motion and for quick starts.

Tail—Like other Northern dogs, the Elkhound carries his tail set high over the back. But the tail differs from some of the others in being tightly curled and carried on the center line. In some instances it is curled one and one-half times; occasionally one finds it curled so tightly that it looks like a knot, which is undesirable. It should not be fan-shaped or loosely curled. Its bone is heavy and evenly tapered, being approximately ten to thirteen inches in length. A tail carried too much to one side is a fault, but not as serious as a loosely curled tail. The tail should be thickly and closely haired without brush, which means that the hair must not be too long or sparse.

T. Hemsen has a very good discussion of the Elkhound tail in *Om Elghunder og Elgjakt i Norge de Siste 50 Ar:*

"The tail is, when correctly rolled and carried, one of the Elkhound's most typical characteristics, and will contribute strongly to give the dog a good appearance. The tail indicates the dog's temperament. If the dog's tail falls backward, it shows weakness and poor nerves. Emphasis should be placed on this fault. A judge shall also try to judge the dog's inner qualities, if possible, with regard to breeding good hunting dogs. The tail's uprolling starts at the tip. The outermost joint sometimes gets so tightly rolled in grown dogs that it makes a crook which cannot be straightened. It may be so tightly curled that the tip is squeezed out to one side, usually to the left, and with a little tuft of black hair to indicate if the dog is right or left tailed. Both are regarded equally. I have often heard it said that a right tailed dog was not purebred, and no good as a hunting dog. I mention this because I want to squelch this old belief. The tail should have the tightest curl that it can have without the tip being forced to either side—also not off-center of the back. If the tail is loosely rolled, the tail ring is large, less pleasing and un-harmonious—fanlike. The tail should have a circular cross section and be relatively short and about the same circumference through-out its whole length. It should lie so firmly on the pelvis, that the hair on the tail is parted at the place where it lies on the pelvis; and the hair on the pelvis is also parted. A good tight tail goes forward from the base or root, making the dog appear short and full of fire. The forward leaning of the tail can also be so strong that the tail presses out to one side and lies more or less horizontally on the back. On the other hand, a tail which leans slightly backward from the root gives the appearance of not lying well on the back and it easily falls down. Furthermore the dog will seem longer."

Coat—The coat of the Elkhound is very important. Its nature is such as to furnish insulation against heat and cold; consequently the dog does not suffer either in winter or summer. The coat is also water resistant. Because it is thick and smooth-lying, snow does not penetrate it. If the coat is dense, glossy, and hard, burrs, seeds, and brambles will not adhere to it, and mud will be shed quickly when dry.

The Elkhound coat, which is double, is composed of the longer and harsher cover hairs dark at the tips, and a lighter wooly under-coat. The hair is longest on the neck, chest, buttocks, the hind side of the forelegs, and the under side of the tail; in other places it is short and even. In texture it should not be too soft or silky, wiry or open. It is not a stand-off coat and should be profuse, straight and without curl. As a rule, the Elkhound has no odor. A male generally sheds once per year and a bitch twice. Because the dog goes defi-nitely out of coat when he sheds, it may be undesirable to show him at that time. There is an old saying that if an Elkhound looks good while shedding, he is a worthy individual.

Color—The most desirable color is silver gray, but not lighter than cream. It should not be platinum or bluish white; neither too dark nor excessively light. Although light fawn is permissible, especially in young dogs, brown, rust, or yellow tints should not be tolerated. There should be even coloring, beautifully blended with long, gray, dark-tipped covering hairs and a somewhat lighter, wooly undercoat.

With regard to color, T. Hemsen says that yellow or brown can be inherited or it can be due to shedding. In the former case where the yellow is uniform to the bottom of the hair, it is a major fault. In the latter case dogs should not be penalized, as the condition is normal. During or just prior to shedding, the coat "dies" and the undercoat becomes yellow. Later the outer part of the hair turns yellow, while the new hair underneath grows in clean and gray. That dogs look better with new coats in full bloom is important in strong bench show competition. With shedding, the outer coat fades and the black color can become reddish brown, especially under the neck. This has nothing to do with sun bleaching, for a clean-colored dog with a new coat holds color even in summer. The shedding period, particularly for older or for sick animals, can last long. A major fault, frequently overlooked, occurs with the ultra-dark dog when he possesses a sparse and brown undercoat, especially on his back.

According to Hemsen, most dogs with normal coloring have dark masks, black ears, and black streaks from the eyes to the roots of the ears. The gray of the head, which is a lighter color than on the body, must be even, not spoiled by spectacles, light cheeks, or light gray around the eyes. The black mask of the foreface grades evenly into the lighter head color. The lower jaw should be black throughout its entire length. The ears should be dark or black, but on some dogs they are light part way up from the ear root. At least the top half of the ear, including the point, should be dark. An all black head, which is not typical, is classed as a major fault, whereas an all light colored head is only a minor fault. Long, dark, stiff feelers are found on the muzzle and eyebrows.

Old dogs often have light hairs on the muzzle due to age. Although pronounced white markings should not appear, a little white on the chest or on the toes is not a serious fault. On the other hand, a white tip on the tail, which seems to be readily inherited, is not desirable.

The mane should be medium gray and the nape of the neck is lighter than the back. Dark gray over the shoulder blades blends into a characteristic lighter band around the body immediately behind the forelegs. This so-called *harness mark,* a vertical stripe approximately two inches wide from withers to elbow points, consists of a light cover coat without dark points on the hairs. These pigment-free hairs are longer and stiffer than the rest of the cover coat. From the rear part of the neck at the withers, another light colored band slopes to the shoulder joint, situated slightly ahead of where a harness would normally lie.

There is a dark gray saddle and a lighter shade over the rear quarters. The outside curl of the tail is light and the inside dark. Also of light coloration are the chest, stomach, and the area around the anus.

Black, soot, or other dark markings on the feet or legs below the knees is a minor fault, which might indicate a throwback to the Black Elkhound or Bearhound of Norway. The light gray of the feet and legs should taper gradually into the darker gray near the body.

Gait—In no part of the breed Standard is the Elkhound gait clarified or explained. As a rule the Norwegian hunters, judges, and experts do not put much emphasis on it. If a dog stands correctly on strong, springy legs, high on his toes, not sluggish or floppy, that is the important thing. In this country too few have made a study of this breed as a hunter and show dog, and have penalized him because of his narrow gait in back. There are some who compare his gait with the best movers in other breeds having longer bodies, little realizing that the short-bodied Elkhound has his own distinctive gait. Breeders in America are constantly trying to produce a short, compact, well-balanced dog. But a short-backed one does not move the same as a long-backed one. Since the Elkhound is built to travel in rough terrain, his body must of necessity be compact.

If he is to survive as a hunter of big game, he must possess the breed's best qualifications. These have been selected through the centuries by nature's process of self-preservation. In the animal kingdom there is no room for the weak, the crippled, and the help-less. Thousands are born each year and thousands die. Only the strong and the healthy live on. Upon those survivors nature has bestowed something extra—they have what it takes! They are the breeding stock of tomorrow.

The Elkhound is not a man-made dog, not formed or squeezed into a certain pattern; he is a free-lance, proven, time-tested big-game hunter. He must not be too big or too small, low-slung or sway-backed, nor too long. He should have a light, easy, effortless run, be quick in his movements, and above all he must be smart. His gait, which is not a fixed style, is a free changing combination run adaptable to rough country.

The well-proportioned Elkhound has straight, free-moving legs that turn neither in nor out. At a walk or slow trot his legs move in four straight lines, best seen in fresh snow or wet sand. The front legs make outside lines, and the hind legs make inside lines parallel to the front ones. The distance between the outside and the inside lines (on either right or left side) might vary depending upon the width of the chest or the dimensions of the hips. Sometimes these lines are very close together.

Frequently a young dog with a narrow chest does not have enough room between the front legs for normal movement of his hind legs. He finds that he has to move one of his hind legs in a path between the front legs, and the other hind leg moves outside either of the front legs. This is a cause of sidewise-gait.

If a dog is bow-legged, or if his hocks turn out (and feet toe in), the hind legs will track in a center line between the front legs, thus showing only three parallel lines of motion. When the dog's hocks turn in (cow-hocks), the feet turn out. In either case, there is lost motion and thrust.

Viewed from the front, the legs should move in straight lines with good (but not maximum) forward reach, should not weave in or out, and there should be no "paddling." The Elkhound's front and hind quarters are not designed for great speed or fully-extended reach, though many Elkhounds are known to go 28 mph. With the Elkhound, it is endurance, rather than speed, that counts.

In full stride he uses the power gallop, not only with full thrust by his hind legs, but also with power from his front legs. When he gallops fast, his hind legs move outside his front legs. On the hunt he often uses a shorter stride, somewhat like a rocking gallop, which seems to be the easiest locomotion for the Elkhound and a gait that he can continue for hours.

The Elkhound has lost some of his flexibility because of the demand that he be short, compact, square and boxy. The aim for a dog as short as possible could lead to stiff and muscle-bound specimens. Contrast this with a light, smooth, springy movement—free and easy with lots of spirit. The borderline for gait has been reached, and we must place more emphasis upon it in the show ring. May the Elkhound in the future continue to be the simple, natural, unspoiled breed that it has always been.

Ch. Stella with four of her litter by Ch. Fjeldheim's Tito. Bred by Herman Berg (Norway) and owned by Runefjell Kennels.

Elkhound bitch with nine puppies. Owned by the Misses Aarbitz of Nes-i-hole, Norway.

12

Growth Chart of Norwegian Elkhound Puppies

On the four pages that follow, I have included a growth chart tracing the development of three Elkhound puppies. They are by Klegglias Storm ex Tyra av Kotofjell, who I imported in whelp from Norway. Norwegian Elkhound breeders may find it interesting to compare the development of their own young stock with that of these puppies.

On the day of the first listing in the chart, March 7, the puppies were one week old.

Date	Jeni (bitch)	Jorgen (dog)	Jutul (dog)
March 7	1 lb., 11 oz.	2 lbs., 10 oz.	2 lbs., 14 oz.
March 10	2 lbs., 12 oz.	2 lbs., 13 oz.	3 lbs., 10 oz.
March 13	2 lbs., 13 oz.	3 lbs.	3 lbs., 10 oz.
March 16	3 lbs., 3 oz.	3 lbs., 5 oz.	3 lbs., 15 oz.
March 19	3 lbs., 13 oz.	4 lbs.	4 lbs., 8 oz.
March 22	4 lbs., 13 oz.	5 lbs., 2 oz.	5 lbs., 7 oz.
March 25	5 lbs., 2 oz.	5 lbs., 8 oz.	6 lbs.
March 28	5 lbs., 7 oz.	6 lbs., 2 oz.	6 lbs., 8 oz.
April 1	6 lbs., 5 oz.	7 lbs.	7 lbs., 7 oz.
April 4	7 lbs., 2 oz.	7 lbs., 9 oz.	8 lbs., 1 oz.
April 7	8 lbs., 4 oz.	8 lbs., 10 oz.	9 lbs., 3 oz.
April 10	9 lbs.	9 lbs., 2 oz.	9 lbs., 7 oz.
April 13	9 lbs., 6 oz.	9 lbs., 8 oz.	10 lbs.
April 16	10 lbs.	10 lbs., 4 oz.	10 lbs., 7 oz.
April 19	10 lbs.	10 lbs., 13 oz.	10 lbs., 15 oz.
April 22	11 lbs.	11 lbs., 2 oz.	11 lbs., 8 oz.
April 25	11 lbs., 6 oz.	11 lbs., 10 oz.	12 lbs.
April 28	12 lbs.	12 lbs., 4 oz.	12 lbs., 10 oz.

Remarks:

Jeni's eyes are partly open.

All crawling and walking. Wobbly.

They are drinking milk mixed with a little honey.

Walking fairly well and playing.

Eating their first deer meat.

Checked for worms. No worms.

Eating deer meat and egg yolks. Appetite good.

Deer meat, bread, egg yolk, bone meal and vitamins.

Next: liver, increase of the bone meal and cod liver oil.

Tyra served bones to her youngsters today, and what a treat it was!

We had our first hike today.

Tyra teaching them how to hunt. They like it.

We had a long hike, up and down the steep hills. Good exercise.

They love to run up and down the long, steep hills.

Date	Jeni (bitch)	Jorgen (dog)	Jutul (dog)
May 1	12 lbs., 8 oz.	12 lbs., 15 oz.	13 lbs.
May 4	13 lbs., 4 oz.	13 lbs., 9 oz.	13 lbs., 12 oz.
May 7	13 lbs., 12 oz.	14 lbs., 10 oz.	14 lbs., 14 oz.
May 10	14 lbs., 6 oz.	15 lbs., 5 oz.	15 lbs., 8 oz.
May 13	15 lbs.	16 lbs., 3 oz.	16 lbs., 6 oz.
May 16	15 lbs., 9 oz.	17 lbs.	17 lbs., 3 oz.
May 19	16 lbs.	17 lbs., 8 oz.	17 lbs., 12 oz.
May 22	17 lbs., 14 oz.	18 lbs., 4 oz.	18 lbs., 1 oz.
May 25	18 lbs.	19 lbs., 2 oz.	19 lbs.
May 28	18 lbs., 12 oz.	20 lbs., 2 oz.	20 lbs., 4 oz.
May 29	19 lbs.	20 lbs., 10 oz.	20 lbs., 15 oz.
June 7			

Remarks:

Mixed a little dog food in with the rest of the food. The puppies did not like it.

Moved the puppies to the big pen. How they love to gallop around.

They are always looking for bones—the bone marrow is a delicacy. Having a wonderful time.

Hiked $1\frac{1}{2}$ miles today. Mixed dog food in the diet. Puppies were tired and hungry. The dog food disappeared.

Mixed dog food in with the rest of the food. They liked it.

The puppies are now three months old, and have had all their shots. They look fine—good coat and color; a wonderful, easy effortless gait, and they are healthy and strong.

From the time the puppies started walking, I would pick them up, carry them about, talk to them and scratch their chests and stomachs. At first they were frightened, but they soon gained confidence and came to like the rides very much. These small touches laid the foundation for developing friendliness and "personality plus" in the puppies.

After the puppies had had their final shots, the neighbors' children were permitted, even encouraged, to come over and play and romp with them. It was amazing how all of these youngsters, puppies and children, got along.

For long hikes, we would put a wide collar on each puppy, with a long clothes-line fastened to the collar. Thus, we were able to allow them a certain amount of freedom and yet keep them under control, not by force, but in a playful way. In this way, we taught them to walk alongside someone, and to come when called.

Tyra had the job of teaching the art of hunting to her offspring—taking the scent of deer tracks, chasing squirrels and chipmunks, and of course, digging for gophers. Tyra was careful to avoid groundhogs and raccoons—they would be too tough for the youngsters.

When the puppies are sold, we require that they have a good home where the mistress of the house likes dogs. This is a first and foremost condition for the enjoyment of a dog by a family. The home must also have a fenced-in backyard. Under no circumstances should a dog be allowed to stand chained all day, barking, and apt to be teased by children, for he may someday tire of it all and start nipping people. It happens over and over again—a dog goes wrong due to a tragic lack of insight and understanding on the part of some owners.

The Norwegian Elkhound has an inbred craving to belong to someone who cares for him. This is the important thing—to make him a happy comrade. When he reaches the age of nine months to a year, he should take on the responsibility of guarding home and property, and learn the fine art of "gentlemanly" behavior. He must be neither dull and lazy-like nor too aggressive. When an Elkhound is old enough for guard duty, but shows no interest, he must be taught. Here is one suggestion on how to go about accomplishing this: Wake him one evening when the family is sitting about, watching television, or reading. Then let one member of the family sneak out the back door, walk to the front door, and start knocking and making much noise. Everyone gets up and hurries to

"The world is so wide, the forest so deep, and I am so young and little, but brave."
—A puppy of the Runefjell Kennels.

Not bad—hold the pose. Ah, but your ears—well, you are young, they will come.

the door, excited and talking loud. The Elkhound will be right there with you, barking loud and clear. After a few of these evening performances, he'll catch on, and from then out will be a good watch-dog.

I am sure that many of the Elkhound's friends will be wondering why I feed my dogs bones. The bones help to keep the teeth strong and clean, and to develop the big, powerful muscles in the snout, and that is a very important thing. A weak muzzle will often look snipey. (Of course, small, sharp bones should never be fed to dogs. They might become lodged in the throat, or splinter and puncture the stomach and intestines. A large knuckle or shin bone should be chosen.)

My enthusiasm for feeding bones started many years ago. Ranvik, imported from Norway in whelp, had had her first litter of puppies, and they were now close to four weeks old. I was using a puppy formula, consisting mainly of baby food, recommended by an expert dog breeder for supplementary feeding of the puppies because Ranvik's milk did not seem to be enough for the young ones. They seemed to always be looking for something else.

One evening Ranvik went out (she was an excellent hunter), and soon came back with a fresh-killed rabbit, and put it right in with her puppies. Of course I scolded Ranvik, and asked her if she was trying to kill her offspring. For a long time she sat trying to figure it all out—looking not at the puppies, but only at me. The next evening she went out and after a bit I opened the door and looked. No dead rabbit this time. I played with the small ones for a time, then turned out the light and went upstairs. Soon I heard a terrible commotion from the whelping box, and hurried down. Ranvik had killed a rabbit, had gobbled it all down, and after coming inside, had vomited it all up. The puppies had a wonderful feast. I decided that Ranvik had more sense than I had. From that time on the puppies consumed lots of rabbits and squirrels, and they turned out to be the healthiest and best-looking Elkhound litter I had ever raised.

I have long been a great admirer of our wildlife creatures. For instance, there is the wolverine (in Norway, *"jerv"*) —what a powerful animal! And such stamina! I know of an incident where an excellent cross-country skier spotted a wolverine on a flat mountain plateau only a half mile in front of him. Having his rifle along, he gave chase. The snow was soft, and so deep that the wolverine, desperately plowing through, had only its head above the white stuff. Yet, in over five hours of swift skiing the hunter was not able to overtake the wolverine, and it disappeared in a rocky mountainside.

I also like the mountain lion, a powerful mammal of the cat family with great strength, wonderful agile movement, and lots of style and class. And the same goes for the bobcat. If we, the breeders of Norwegian Elkhounds, in our endless search for the superb specimen, could produce some of the best combinations to be found in these wild creatures, we really would have something! These animals are free from hip dysplasia, night blindness, and undershot or overshot jaws. And remember, when they kill for food, they not only eat the meat but also the bones. It takes strong jaws and excellent teeth to pull, tear and tug the meat from the bones of their prey. If these animals did not have proper bites, it would be impossible to get the meat torn to pieces. Where their jaws are not perfect, Nature always has a way to correct the mistake.

Thus, when I see my dogs with both paws on a bone, and pulling or tearing the meat apart, I know the bite is going to be all right. I have never had an Elkhound with a bad bite. But of course, I never give my dogs bones until after they have been well fed.

Note: The puppy Jeni was purchased by Dr. Barbara Burke, and has a wonderful home. Dr. Burke was very active in the Norwegian Elkhound Association of Minnesota a few years back, and was the prime mover in arranging the first International Norwegian Elkhound Convention in 1959 at Minneapolis. With Jeni's excellent bloodlines it should not take Dr. Barbara Burke long to breed some fine Norwegian Elkhounds. She has the interest, and also the place for them.

A lovely handful of Crafdal puppies.

13

The Norwegian Elkhound Personality

I N his *Elghunder og Elgjaks,* Rolf Dammann includes this revealing depiction of an Elkhound personality trait:

A characteristic behavior manifests itself in *Elghunds* at the age of from three to four months, and often becomes more intense as time goes on. This is that he is so easily offended by his owner.

The young *Elghund* can stand lots of abuse from other dogs, and even if somebody throws stones at him it does not bother him much. He shakes himself and all is soon forgotten. He is quickly back to normal, friendly and happy.

But let his owner give him a smart blow, or even just scold him in a harsh manner—and it is a different thing altogether. Our young dog becomes terribly offended, and it can last for many days.

Perhaps the owner and dog have been out for an evening walk. The dog has done something wrong, and as a result has been scolded, or even slapped, and then put in the enclosure. As far as the owner is concerned, this ends the matter, and all is forgotten. But not so with the *Elghund.*

When the owner comes out to greet his friend the next morning, the dog that would ordinarily respond in good cheer, wagging his tail and jumping up against the fence, instead turns away from the fence with his tail hanging down and his head low. He has not forgotten last night's happening, and is still deeply insulted. He will not touch the food; it just stands there. If he receives a pat, he may move his tail a little, but he never looks his owner in the eye. He only stands. The owner wonders if he is sick; but no, he looks healthy. So finally, the owner has no choice but to leave him standing there. By afternoon, he may be over the insult. But sometimes it may be a day or more before he will forgive and forget.

I know of an *Elghund* that crawled under a barn and lay there for three days before the ordeal was forgotten. Mr. Theodore Bache relates a story of famous Gamle Bamse Gram that happened in the Frydenlund Hotel in Slidre. A German woman was warmly admiring the dog, whose fantastic hunting prowess had not only been proven with many *elg*, but also many bear. She asked for permission to pat Bamse. "Why sure," answered his owner, "so long as I am around, it certainly would be safe."

But Bamse had other ideas, and snapped and growled at the lady. It was the only time I ever saw Consule Gram slap Gamle Bamse. His pride hurt, Bamse crawled under a sofa. His owner, remorseful, in very tender voice begged Bamse to come out and forget the incident. But it was no use. It was a couple of hours before Bamse would come out, and it took many days before he could completely forgive and forget the insult from his owner.

Was it just this dog himself, Bamse, evidencing this almost human feeling, or was it something in his makeup from way back? We don't know, of course. But it seems that the *Elghund* that is his owner's most devoted friend, the one that has the best home, the best treatment—is the one most likely to be wounded and insulted by unjust humiliation.

A thought is that it may trace back to when the Norwegian Elkhound was more than just a companion. Of old he was a free-born hunter, a very important member of the big game hunting team. For those folk, he was the difference between a good plentiful life and a scanty existence. If the game was there, he would find it. He was a noble and proud hunting comrade. He knew his part and played it well. He also knew that on the *elg* hunt, a false move or mistake would leave him a dead dog. But he never hesitated—he would give all for his man, and expected in turn that his man would give all for him. It was a fifty-fifty proposition.

There is also in the Norwegian Elkhound an independence that may likewise stem back to the days when he was the one that was depended upon—the "bring-home-the-bacon" fellow.

This fierce independence and pride appears to have been well-exampled in the Honorable William H. Timbers' great Ch. Leif of Dragondell, C.D.S., T.D.

Leif, the only champion Norwegian Elkhound to ever achieve the Tracking title, was tragically killed by a car in front of the Timbers' home. More than 200 letters of sympathy were received—among them letters from a Justice of the Supreme Court of the United States, the Governor of Connecticut, a former Governor of Vermont, the executive vice-president of the American Kennel Club, and innumerable prisoners, jurors, court personnel, and the entire federal judiciary of Connecticut, Vermont and New York.

In a touching tribute to Leif, which appeared in the Norwegian Elkhound Association of America Newsletter of December, 1966, Judge Timbers revealed the personality that helped make this dog so colorful:

"His loss is like that of a member of the family . . . Those of you who came to know Leif will share with us many happy memories of this Norwegian Elkhound who epitomized so well the admirable qualities of the "Dog of the Vikings": beauty, intelligence, loyalty, rugged independence, and an abiding love of mankind.

"I have thought so many times during the past two weeks, since his tragic death, of the question you so often kiddingly asked, as to whether Leif or I would ultimately win out in the 'battle of the U.D.'. In many ways, as I reflect back upon the running battle Leif and I had during the past three years over this matter, there is no question in my mind that he completely outsmarted me. He knew the routine perfectly. One obedience judge after another commented that Leif could have gone in the ring and have compiled a near-perfect score without any handler at all. But he was just plain determined not to surrender his independence. In short, he wanted it known that, Utility degree or no Utility degree, he was first, last and always a Norwegian Elkhound at heart. And so it was.

"You probably are familiar with Lorenz' *King Solomon's Ring* in which he refers to this characteristic of the lupus dog as follows: 'He will lay down his life for his master, but will never give up his independence.' Leif must have read that at some point; or did he have to?"

Ch. Leif of Dragondell, C.D.X, T.D., pictured in harness on the day he won his tracking degree, September 9, 1961. At left, Leif is pictured taking the high jump while training for his C.D.X. degree. Owned by the Hon. William H. Timbers of Darien, Conn.

Gray Norwegian Elkhound

DRIV AV KOTOFJELL

Whelped May 26, 1964
NKK #64/6069 - Norwegian Show Champion
                Norwegian Hunting Champion
SKKR #14573/66 - Swedish Show Champion
                 Swedish Hunting Champion
DSK #302885W - Danish Show Champion

Norsk Gullhund 1966 (Best in all-breed inter-
      national dog show, NKK, 1966)
International Champion, 1966

                    Bamse (3084)
              Trym (57/2360)
                    Topsy av Suteras (54/2533)
        Klegglias Storm (61/3342)
                    Troll (1330Ø)
              Tyra (58/79)
                    Bringa (552V)
INT. CH. DRIV AV KOTOFJELL
                    Bjonn (56/392)
              Tufsen av Kotofjell (58/4731)
                    Elgi (56/4804)
        Lotte av Kotofjell (61/7943)
                    Ch. Storm (54/1359)
              Tussi (58/4422)
                    Tussi av Suteras (641Ø)

Breeder: Birger Grønvold (Norway)
Original Owner: Reidar Stromme (Norway)
Present Owner: Werner Andersson (Sweden)

172

Driv av Kotofjell, Norway's most famous dog of today.

14

The Lady or the Hunter—Whither the Norwegian Elkhound?

THE huntsmen were the first to recognize and admire a well-built, well-suited hunting dog. Through the years, man's love for hunting has been in his heart and soul. To hunt with a good dog has always been a thrill, and it takes on an extra pride when the dog is a handsome one. It is therefore logical to assume that these sportsmen were the first to compare the various breeds and individual dogs as to their good and bad points, and in so doing they acted as forerunner to our modern dog shows.

The hunters' view was that the dog must be typical, sound and suited to the terrain. He must be a tireless hunter, and above all, a handsome and easily-groomed house dog.

Men with knowledge and experience in hunting composed the Norwegian Elkhound standard, a simple and easily understood description of an ideal big game hunter. For over half a century, the Elkhound standard has undergone very little change. It was written first and foremost from the sportsmen's and hunters' point of view, with prime concern for an excellent hunting dog. At the same time, it recognized that the Elkhound must be handsome enough to challenge any other breed in the show ring.

Therefore he who would really know the standard and judge the Norwegian Elkhound, must remember that behind the standard looms the fields, the forests, and the wilderness. There is the Elkhound's realm—there is where he belongs. If the breeder-owners and judges have long experience in big-game hunting they will, as a rule, have the eye for the correct type. They know what it takes.

Unhappily, some years ago, people in this country originated a new concept for the breed—"The Norwegian Elkhound must be short, compact, square, and heavy-boned." As a result, a new type of Elkhound appeared. He had somewhat short legs, looking like a roly-poly, with open coat and often—a swayback. The light, springy stride, the wonderful Elkhound gait, also disappeared.

We do have some dedicated folk who are defending and guarding the hunting type, and with so many recent imports from Norway we may yet be able to stem the tide. The Elkhound owners and breeders have a long and cumbersome road ahead—a great struggle to get back on the right track. We must educate not only the judges, but also the public, to the correct hunting type, the Elkhound called for in the standard. We are becoming short-handed in experts in the field of big-game hunting, but so long as we recognize the shortcomings and keep the self-appointed experts who would lead us astray in their proper place, we can make it.

An important difference between Norwegian Elkhound fanciers here and abroad is that in Norway they are 99% men—hunters, field and show judges—and in America, 90% of the breeders and owners are women. It is one of the mysteries of our time how the world's finest big game hunter came to be adopted by the ladies in this land.

If the Elkhound had been promoted as a popular hunting dog, he would of course have had much better protection, and we would have only one type of Elkhound—the original one.

But let's face it, the ladies of this land are now in the driver's seat. In their hands rests the fate of the Norwegian Elkhound in America. In my travels around this country, I have visited hundreds of breeders and owners, and have found them intelligent, eager to learn, and interested in improving the breed. If the ladies decide that they are going to breed the hunting type, nothing will stop them—they will move mountains to reach their objective.

But they must guard against the saboteurs. We do have some

scissors-happy jokers in some parts of our land who cannot leave the Elkhound alone. They cut the whiskers (feeling hairs) and often trim the coat, and still have the nerve to call the alteration a hunting dog.

On a hunt the Elkhound must close his eyes when he goes through thick underbrush or high weeds. If not, his eyes would be full of burrs and seeds. He must use his feeling hairs (whiskers) to find his way through, and without the whiskers he would soon have a bloody nose. I will support a paragraph in the standard stating that if whiskers are trimmed, the Elkhound must be removed from the show ring. It would be one way to stop this nuisance.

Kaisa av Tallo, rated by Olav Campbell as "the best bitch I ever had."

Elkhounds with a record set of Alaskan moose antlers. Owned by Mr. and Mrs. Robert Smolley, and photo by Mr. Smolley.

15

The Elg (Moose)

by Olav Campbell, Norway

THE Moose is our noblest wild big game. He is the King of the Forest. No one who has seen a full-grown bull moose standing with his head lifted high, and the sun shining on the majestic horns, will ever forget the sight.

On a quiet walk in the woods of an early morning, one will often find the moose feeding in the marshes, or standing at a small lake, eating water lilies.

The moose varies much in size and weight. The bull moose can weigh (dressed weight) from 200 to over 300 kilograms, which roughly translates into 400 to over 600 pounds. His body and neck are short and powerful, and the legs are long and sturdy. The head is quite long, with a big, wide nose.

Only the bull has horns, and they are of considerable variation in size and form. Some have shovel horns, others have open racks like the elk.

The hunters, of course, prefer the shovel horns. If the rack is of good size, they are most impressive. The bull moose begins to grow horns at the age of one, and as a rule he has only one point in the first year. By the fall, he is shedding the single point. The horns are shed every late fall and winter, but toward spring, a new rack starts growing.

At first the horns are of soft substance, but they become hard as rock when full grown. The moose gets one point added to the rack every year, and the horn gets stronger and more impressive as the years go by. When the bull gets old, the rack retreats and gets smaller each year, so it is hard to judge the bull's age by the horn. Checking his teeth is the surest way to determine his age.

The horns are used as weapons, particularly during the breeding season in the fall when the bulls fight a terrific battle in competition for the cow. Some hunters claim that the bull with the open rack (elk horn) is always the winner.

In a fight against other animals, the bull uses his front hoofs. He leaps forward and at the same time slams his hoofs down like sledge hammers, with his full weight behind them. It is a fearsome weapon and many an Elkhound has been killed on a moose hunt.

In the fall, when the bull moose is on the run in constant search of cows in season, he often digs shallow holes in the ground, and lets his urine in them. There is always a very strong odor from these holes. The meeting place for the bull and the cow has thus been established.

With all the fighting, the bull loses lots of weight each fall, and after a bit becomes thin. The moose meat at this time will often have a bitter taste.

When it is calfing time for the cow, she selects a place where she has good protection against the wind and weather, plus a good view of the surrounding territory. As a rule, the calf is born in May or June, but he can be born as early as April and as late as August.

The pregnancy for the cow is 9 months. She usually has her first calf in her third year. There is generally only one calf, but later twins or triplets can be born. After a short time, the newly-born calf will be able to follow his mother in her wanderings. If some other creatures come too close to the cow's territory when the calf is young, the mother will attack the intruder. At birth, the calf has a red-brown color, which will turn gray in fall or winter. He grows very fast, but if his mother is shot accidentally in the fall, he will have a hard time surviving the tough winter.

The calf will follow his mother for a year. But if she becomes pregnant again, and is within calfing time, she will then chase the yearling away.

The most common territory for the moose is the pine and fir country, but he often wanders to higher ground in the summer, sometimes even going above the timberline. Here he feeds on willow and mountain ash along creeks and small lakes. His main food is brush, twigs, and leaves of aspen and birch.

Newborn **moose** calf.

Trygg av Skromtefjell, owned by Sigurd Vik.

16

The Hunting Norwegian Elkhound

THE name Norwegian Elkhound is somewhat misleading in that the dog does not hunt elk (wapiti), nor is he technically a Hound. In Norway the Norsk Elghund, as he is called, is used primarily as a hunting dog for big game. Since *elg* refers to a member of the moose family and *hund* is the common European word for dog, the term "moose dog" would seem more appropriate. Sometimes he is referred to as the *graa dyrehund,* which may be translated as the gray big-game dog. No game is too big or too small for this dog of the Vikings. He is equally adept at hunting moose, bear, mountain lion, wolf, fox, rabbit, and even upland birds.

When one appreciates that the Norwegian elk is essentially the same as our large American moose, and when one realizes that as many as 40,000 *elg* are shot in the Scandinavian countries per year, mostly with the help of Elkhounds, then will the Elkhound assume his true significance as a sporting dog.

To find moose in Norway's endless forests without a dog would be well nigh hopeless.

To understand and appreciate this clever dog, it would be advisable to see him in action in his native *fjells* and forests. There he is in his glory!

The hunting season, which starts late in September, lasts only five to ten days. It is absolutely necessary that the dog be in top condition to stand the strenuous run from sunrise to sunset each day of the short season. Having selected a likely place to hunt, you take your dog there. What a picture he makes as he stands like a statue, high on his toes, head up, ears pricked forward and nostrils taking scent through the clear mountain air! His brown eyes peer into the dense forest. His silver coat shines. Every muscle is tense and ready to spring.

Then he is off on the hunt. His movements are quick and noise-less. You start moving in a fairly straight line, always against the wind. Your dog must cover all the territory on both sides of your path, which means in and out through the brush, stumps, stones, and windfalls. It means a steady run, not fast, because the area must be hunted thoroughly, but a half run, half fast walk referred to as *dilt*. Although you may not see the dog for a while, he will be constantly crossing and recrossing your path—sort of reporting to you. Ultimately, he will find a moose track or will catch the direct scent of the animal itself, and then may disappear for a long period.

You stand on a high point and listen for the baying (*los*) to commence which will indicate that your dog has his quarry at bay. His rhythmic notes in the distance stir and thrill you. As you run toward the sounds, you wonder about the moose. Perhaps it is a wise old bull—or it may be a scared young one. Will the moose stay and fight? Or will he run? After a while you stop, open-mouthed, heart pounding, hand behind the ear listening. The stand is closer now. Soon you are on the run again. The knapsack on your back is bouncing up and down. The coffee kettle is rattling. But you do not notice these things. You are thinking of your pal out there, all alone with no one to help him. He is such a small thing against such a big brute.

Think of all the deathtraps into which a smart moose could lure the dog; for instance, thick underbrush where a dog cannot spring aside when the moose strikes with his knife-sharp hoofs, hard as rocks. You can imagine, too, how those massive horns can tear things to shreds.

Another deathtrap is the shallow fjord, where the moose has the dog at a definite disadvantage. While the moose with his long legs wades out into the water, the dog must swim, his progress slower. Under these conditions the moose can turn quickly, seize the dog on his wide antlers, and toss him in the air or trample him to death.

Your thoughts wander to a third trap, the narrow ledge on a mountain precipice, vertical walls on one side and the endless deep on the other, where the sure-footed moose will balance step by step and the low-creeping Elkhound will follow closely. Here is a chance for the moose to put an end to the dog with a sudden stop and a swift kick.

After hours that seem like days, you catch a glimpse through the pines of the two opponents facing each other on the stand, the Elkhound appearing even smaller in comparison with his huge adversary. No wonder the moose is called the "King of the Forest!" When he comes crashing through the woods, higher than a horse, head outstretched, his heavy antlers ripping big branches right and left and knocking over small trees like bowling pins, he is tremendous! Even seasoned hunters tremble when he unexpectedly comes thundering through the brush. He is hot-tempered and ugly when wounded or trapped, majestic and noble when he raises his great head with lofty horns for his last look over his kingdom.

No other hunting may be compared with moose hunting. You and your dog are pitted against the forest, the mountain, and the river. The sport requires teamwork between man and dog. Both must be in top physical condition to endure. For this work the dog should possess a keen nose, great courage, a powerful, agile body, well developed chest, and short back. One can readily understand why these points are emphasized in the Elkhound Standard.

The most remarkable part of moose hunting in Norway is that even the top ranking show Elkhounds are expected to participate in the sport. If they cannot hunt, they are considered worthless as far as breeding is concerned, and cannot become champions.

Moose hunting, which is far from easy, requires outstanding qualities in the dog. He must have at least four special traits: first, he must have a good nose; second, steady nerves; third, a deep, long-range voice; and fourth, he must be smart. The dog must take scent of the big game from a long distance and be able to differentiate between moose, bear, and other animals.

If the Elkhound is nervous, high-strung, and hot tempered, he should not be used for moose hunting. It would be a waste of time to spend months training such a dog. The natural-born hunter gives the best results.

When the dog has a moose at bay in the distance and his voice is high pitched and squeaky, the hunter cannot hear the baying and will not know where the stand is. Consequently, many an otherwise good Elkhound is of little use as a *loshund*, though he may prove satisfactory as a *bandhund*. The former ranges freely on his own to locate game and hold it at bay. The latter operates in a harness with a twenty-foot leash, which is attached to the hunter's belt. When trailing a moose, the *bandhund* must avoid obstacles such as windfalls and low-hanging branches that would greatly hinder the hunter. This dog trails the moose until he approaches fairly close to his quarry. Then the hunter ties the Elkhound to a tree and proceeds to find and kill the moose.

The experienced hunter is greatly concerned with the dog's performance on the hunt. Some qualities the dog inherits, but others he must be smart enough to learn. On the trail, he must know if the track is too old, or if the moose has traveled at a rapid pace, in which case it probably would be in some distant valley at the time. As a rule, the Elkhound will not try to take scent in the low areas between the ridges, because he knows that the air currents do not often follow the contour of the land. Instead, he will be observed on the hills taking scent. Sometimes he even stands on his hind legs so as to reach higher in the breeze.

It is a critical moment when he has found the moose. A good dog will take his time on the approach. He must then decide whether the moose is old or young, or if it is a cow with a calf. When it is an old one and not too scared, the approach is more direct. The dog tries a small "woof." If nothing happens, he increases the volume and moves in closer. Soon he makes a pass at the big bull and then a fight may follow.

In the case of a young moose, the dog should proceed with caution so as to avoid scaring it into headlong flight. Should the moose not stand, the dog must follow silently, for if he bays the moose will run faster and farther. A mute dog may get another chance to hold the quarry when it stops. The dog should not pursue, however, when the game goes at too fast a pace.

The Elkhound is especially useful in locating a wounded moose. This requires keen scenting ability, courage, and perseverance. It is the law in Norway that hunters must wait approximately two hours after wounding a moose before proceeding to track him down and kill him.

Although bears are not as numerous as they formerly were in the Scandinavian countries, they still are hunted with dogs. As in moose hunting, the bear is trailed by Elkhounds and held at bay by barking and by nipping at its heels. Sometimes the bear is kept at bay for hours by one dog or two dogs.

For hunting black cock, *tiur, capercaille,* and other upland birds that flush into trees, the Elkhound is quite proficient. But pointing and retrieving birds are not his forte.

In concluding this chapter on the hunting Elkhound, it is our hope that the group referred to as sports hunters will increase from year to year. These men know that it is a privilege and honor to hunt in field and forest on a beautiful autumn day just for the sport of hunting. They do not count the result in dollars, but in happy memories that go on and on. Never to be forgotten are the evenings spent in some secluded cabin where the Elkhounds stretch out on the floor in the flickering glow of the fireplace, where glasses are lifted in toasts to happy field trial and show winners, where stories of the hunt are told and retold, and where friends unite in a fellowship that warms each hunter's heart and soul.

Elgstolens Buster and Elgstolens Jerv.

17

Elghund Field Trial in Norway

by Dr. Jesper Hallingby, Norway

THE *Elghund* was originally a hunting dog, and is still very much so in its native Norway. While some are farm dogs, and some watchdogs or pets, the majority are used for hunting.

In contrast to America, dogs are still permitted to take part in big game hunting in Norway. In fact, not only are they permitted, but laws are constantly being proposed that would *require* every hunting team to have dogs, to use in finding wounded animals.

Elg hunting in Norway is thus done mainly with dogs—either free-ranging (*loshund*), or on leash. The loose dog tries to find the *elg* on its own, either by open scent or by tracking it down. When it finds the *elg*, the dog barks and tries to keep the prey at bay until the hunter arrives and kills it. The leashed dog, on the other hand, is led by the hunter. The dog tries to find the *elg* in the same way as the *loshund*, by scent or tracking. When the *elg* is located, the hunter approaches (always against the wind) until he is near enough to the animal to see and shoot it.

Which of the two hunting methods is used depends upon the local circumstances. The loose dog is used where there are large, dense forests. But in terrain where the forestation is more sparse, with big open bogs or mountain area, the leashed dog is employed.

To find the best hunting dogs, so that they may be used for

breeding, annual field trials have been established at terrains all over the country. There is no question that an enthusiasm for hunting and many of the other inner qualities that make for a good hunting dog are hereditary, as much as are the readily seen exterior qualities. However, it is more difficult to breed the hunting qualities. It is hoped that study of the results of the field trials will prove a helpful guide for such breeding.

The field trials provide other benefits, too. For one, there is the financial aspect. An award at a hunting test immediately increases the value of a dog for sale, or as a breeding dog.

But for most field trial participants, it is the sheer sport of the tests that counts most—the urge to compete and show what one has. The opportunity of "hunting" for several days in such ideal terrains —with large *elg* stock and most attractive surroundings—is highly prized. And along with an expert judgment on one's dog, it provides a most enjoyable get-together with other eager hunters and dog lovers.

As far as we know, such tests for *Elghunds* are held only in Norway, Sweden and Finland. The rules for the tests vary in each country.

We were rather slow to start field trial competition with our *Elghunds* in Norway—much later than with tests for Beagles and bird dogs. The reason was that it is difficult to find terrains large enough and suitable for *Elghund* field trials. An attempt to test a couple of dogs was made in 1916–1917. Then it was not until 1948 that we, with the initiative furnished by Erik Enberg, Sven Mjaerum, Reidar Stromme and myself, started the so-called field trial for *Elghunds* in the Vang forests. Mjaerum and Enberg placed their hunting terrain at our disposal. Here we gained the experience needed to formulate the Field Trial Rules that have since been in effect.

G. A. Treschow and Harald Lovenskiold have let us use their large forest properties at Fritzoe Verk and Nordmarken for tests. In recent years, the terrains in Nannestad, Orje, Hoff in Vestfold and Faaberg have been used with good results. Tests have also been conducted in the Verdalsbruket forests in North Trondelag.

We have now come so far with the field trials that the Norsk Kennel Klub has decided that a hunting test award be required before an *Elghund* may become a champion. Recently, we have also established a hunting championship, requiring two First Prizes at hunting tests in two different years. It is also an established principle that the tests should be as close to regular hunting as possible. The only difference is that in the tests that the dog has to be baying and holding the *elg* at bay a specified time before he is called in and leashed.

A field trial is performed in this manner:

The night before the test, the participants meet with dogs and judges at the headquarters. The conductor of the test has a meeting with the judges, and the needed number of terrains are drawn up on the map. The aim is to make the terrains as alike in every way as possible, including the number of *elg* inhabiting them.

Each judge is assigned a separate terrain, which is under his control throughout the test. The dogs are tested for two days, and are entitled to at least six hours of testing each day. They are tested by a different judge, in a different terrain, each day. This obviously helps assure a fairer judgment.

Early in the first test day, breakfast is served. Then the trainer with the test dogs and the judge leave for their specific terrain, in the direction that the judge—taking the wind into consideration—deems best.

If an unleashed dog *(loshund)* is being tested, the judge orders the dog to be let loose right away. The judge will immediately note the starting move *(utslaget)* of the dog. It is very important the dog start well and show that it is definitely setting out to find *elg*.

When the dog tracks down the *elg*, and starts for it, the judge and the trainer watch developments at a distance. If the *elg* runs and the dog follows, the men have to try to keep up with them. When standing baying *(staa-los)* occurs, the men take position against the wind so as to be able to hear without scaring the *elg*. When the dog has been baying continually for an hour and a half or more, the baying period needed to qualify for a First Prize, the judge will normally carefully position himself close enough so that he can be sure that it really is an *elg*, and to study the behavior of the dog in front of the *elg*. Then the trainer tries to call the dog in order to leash it. In most cases it is difficult because the dog feels encouraged by the presence of its master, and—particularly if the *elg* gets scared —becomes still more eager and insistent. However, if the dog is easily recalled, it is a plus for him in the judge's book. Sooner or later the dog will be back, and can be tried again at tracking and then on another *elg*. It counts much in its favor if the dog is cool and collected at the start *(rolig uttak)* so that it does not scare the *elg*, but instead actually calms it down.

The interest of the dog in other game or animals must not be so intense as to disturb the hunting. Its enthusiasm for hunting must be great enough that it will not give up, but will work all dog—if necessary—to find *elg*. And the dog must be eager enough to hold the *elg* at bay, lest it take off at great speed and disappear completely.

The dog's barking may vary very much. Some take it easy—others keep going loud and clear all the time. However, it is the conduct of the dog that by and large really influences the behavior of the *elg*. The sound of the barking identifies whether the dog is dealing with a calm animal or not. The judge has to consider all of this in determining whether the *Elghund* is to be recommended for First, Second, or Third Prize—or no award at all.

In the tracking field trial, the dog is in harness all day. Out in the terrain, the trainer keeps against the wind as much as possible until the dog finds tracks fresh enough to be of interest, or until it gets the scent of *elg*. In tracking, the dog should guide the trainer speedily and surely to the *elg*, without letting anything distract him. The dog should clearly indicate when it is close to the animal, soundlessly approach, and be absolutely quiet and silent all the time. The dog should not react to shots, and should possess an eagerness for hunting strong enough to keep him working all day to find *elg* without interest for other game or domestic animals. The award system is the same as for the unleashed *(loshund)* dogs.

Following the test, all documents are forwarded to the Norsk Kennel Klub to be studied and evaluated by the Field Trial Committee, which then presents its recommendations. The final decision is up to the Board of the Kennel Club.

I would like to point out a few things in connection with the test results up to now. It is often heard at dog shows that "show dogs" cannot be used for hunting. To qualify for the field trial test, an *Elghund must have first received an award at a show*. So while the test does not furnish a measure between "show dogs" and "non-show dogs," its results do prove that "show dogs" can hunt and hunt well. The remarkable fact is that of all the dogs tested up to now, and awarded First Prize, *more than 2/3 had also received First*

Prizes at shows. A beautiful exterior does not prevent the dog from becoming a good hunter.

(The exterior standard for *Elghunds* has been worked out with an eye to the fact that it is a hunting dog. It is therefore important that this standard be maintained in the judging at the shows, and that the dog is not permitted to become too big and heavy. In countries where the dog is not employed for hunting, there is an unfortunate tendency in this direction.)

Another result of the tests has been to prove that the old discrimination against the bitches *(tisper)* is, to put it mildly, absolutely unfounded. The tests prove untrue the claim that bitches are unsuitable as unleashed *(loshund)* dogs.

Furthermore, it is noticeable that the temperament of the *Elghund* is completely different today from what it was a few years ago. It was an old theory that an *Elghund* had to be ill-tempered if used as a hunting dog. So they were at that time. Today, most of them are good-natured and friendly, and easily handled in the show rings or the woods during field trials, wherever competing. Nor has this caused any sacrifice of their hunting qualities.

It is still too early to decide what influence the field trials have had in the breeding of *Elghunds*. In a few years, we will know much better. Generally, the breeders have been selecting good test dogs as breeding dogs. What can happen when a pair really clicks together is proven by a litter sired by the well-known Elgstoelens Fanto ex Vera av Flisefyr. Both dogs were excellent working dogs. Fanto was known as one of the best *Elghunds* in the country, with two First Prizes in field trials, and one award as top dog of the test. Out of a litter of seven puppies, born June 23, 1955, three won First Prize awards at hunting tests: Boss av Flisefyr, 56/913; Bill av Flisefyr, 56/910; and Buster av Flisefyr, 56/912. A fourth brother, Tass av Flisefyr, was as good as the others, but due to an exterior flaw, was not exhibited, and therefore did not qualify to take the test. A fifth, a bitch, is an excellent working dog. The sixth, also a bitch, was also good but was not used too much. Only the seventh puppy did not become a hunting dog. A truly remarkable litter of hunting dogs!

A field trial is, in a sense, a graduation. There will always be an element of chance involved. The dog may be unlucky and encounter very difficult animals, the weather may be bad, or the dog may simply be indisposed the day the tests are held. On the other hand, the dog may well outdo any previous effort. The important thing is that the owner be sportsman enough to take victory or defeat in the right spirit. If he does, he will find the hunting test days to be among the most eventful of the Fall for him.

For quick reference, here is an extract of the hunting test rules of the Norsk Kennel Klub:

10. The judge must have a special book during the test. He notes down the weather, the condition of the terrain, the temperature and a calculation of the *elg* population in the field. He also observes the dog during the test, when unleashed or leashed, the exact baying time, its behavior in the terrain and to the *elg* and behavior before, during, and after the baying. The judge must carefully note exact time and place where another dog is heard in order to, if necessary, supplement the impression of the fellow judge. If the judge hears baying coming into his test sector which might be coming from the test dog of another participant, the judge must, if possible, leash his test dog if it has not already found the *elg*. All in all, the judge must make notes of everything of interest during the test. Based on his observations the judge answers the following points:
   a. The hunting eagerness of the dog.
   b. Interest in finding *elg*.
   c. Contact and cooperation with the trainer—obedience.
   d. Quiet and calm when he approaches the *elg*.
   e. Ability to stop the *elg*.
   f. Bark and usage of it.
   g. Determination in holding the *elg*.
   h. Tracking.
   i. Interest in other game and domestic animals.
   j. Recommendation for prize degree.
11. To be awarded First Prize—Unleashed (*Loshund*)—the following is required:
   1. He must show extremely good hunting eagerness, with an ease in running and searching for the *elg* in the forest, without losing contact with the trainer.
   2. The dog must have a good loud voice and use it sensibly.
   3. He must have a sensible calm approach toward the *elg* and good ability to stop the *elg* from moving away.
   4. He must hold the *elg* at bay at least 1½ hours. He must also be tried in contact with other *elg*.
      If the *elg* decides to move, the dog must aim to stop him. But the *Elghund* must be silent—no barking. He must be ready to track and trail the *elg*, even in his own tracks.

To be awarded Second Prize as *Loshund,* the following is required:
   1. He must show extremely good hunting eagerness, and must thoroughly search the territory for *elg* tracks and *elg* without losing contact with the trainer.

2. The *Elghund* must have a good loud voice.

3. He must have a sensibly calm approach toward the *elg*.

4. He must have at least one hour constant stand, holding the *elg*, and also be tried on other *elgs*. If the *elg* moves off, the dog must try to stop him but must not bark. He also must be willing to re-track his own footmarks.

To be awarded Third Prize as *Loshund* the following is required:

1. A good practical *loshund* must have good hunting interest and make a wide search looking for *elg* and *elg* footprints, and should not lose contact with the trainer.

2. He must have a good loud voice and must hold the *elg* at bay at least ½ hour.

3. He must try to hold the *elg* back if the animal decides to move on.

4. He should also be able to track and trail.

5. He must not leave the *elg* in the stand before the time is up (this is of course a rule for all *loshunds*) .

6. If the trainer is some distance away, the dog must at least report once (keep in touch with the trainer) .

For all prize categories it is required that the dog not leave the standing animal before the baying period required for the prize degree has run out. A single report is permitted if the trainer is a considerable distance away.

12. Hunting tests for leashed dogs:

A leashed dog shall have harness and must never be let loose during the test. The dog's job is to locate the *elg* in the terrain as fast as possible and lead the hunter to it. The dog must show that it works consciously to find *elg*. The dog must be completely silent and never bark or whine. It must not pull so strongly in the leash that it groans or coughs and must be able to move soundlessly across the grounds. Normally it should not follow the *elg* track slavishly but work with head high in order to scent the *elg*. The dog should utilize the terrain and the wind sensibly. If the dog is in doubt about the location of the *elg* the trainer may lead the dog back with the wind before proceeding anew. The dog shall clearly mark when the *elg* is near. If the dog works on *elg* track, it should not be blamed if it leaves the track and closes in on other *elgs* which are nearer, and it is a plus for the dog if it prefers a bull *elg*. It is not a drawback if the dog passes a cow in order to head directly for a bull. The dog should be able to follow the track of a wounded *elg* (blood track) without being distracted by other tracks or animals. The dog should not be blamed if it covers shorter distances to fowl or other animals if it does not work on *elg*, but exaggerated interest in other animals is not permissible. It is a plus for the dog if it exclusively concentrates on *elg*. When shooting occurs the dog should not pull hard in such a way that it makes it difficult to fire more shots. It should not react in such a way that it will not work any more after shots are fired.

13. For First Prize for leashed dogs, the following is required:

Dog showing superior ability to locate *elg* fast and surely, and faultlessly takes the hunter to the animal.

For Second Prize for leashed dogs, the following is required:
Dog showing very good ability to locate the *elg* and without serious faults takes the hunter to the animal.
For Third Prize for leashed dogs, the following is required:
Dog shows generally good ability to locate the *elg* and without faults of importance to the result of the hunt takes the hunter to the animal.
14. A general rule for all dogs is that they must not be scared of shots, and must not show such interest in other game and cattle that it disturbs the *elg* hunt.

Moose killed in Murudalen in 1946.

18

A Norwegian Field
Trial Report

FOLLOWING is an account of a typical Norwegian field trial, as reported on pages 137 and 138 in *Om Elghunder og Elkjakt i Norge de Siste 50 Ar.* The work of the now famous hunter, Elgstolens Jerv, is described.

"FIELD TRIAL FOR ELKHOUNDS (LOOSE) IN N. VANGS DISTRICT, SEPTEMBER 26, 1949

Leader: Sven Mjearum
Judges: Olaf Afkjaernand and Sigurd Hole
Dog's Name: Elgstolens Jerv, 5 years
Owner and Handler: E. V. Enberg, Oslo
Weather Conditions Wind: Southwest
                    Morning Temperature: 11° C.
                    Noon Temperature: 18° C.
                    Light haze until 9 A.M.
                    Trial terrain height from 575 to 900 meters.

"We went from Lavlia by automobile to Bringebu eight miles away. Jerv was on leash going west from Bringebu toward the Furnes district. At 7:09 A.M. about 500 yards from Furnes, he was turned loose. From the very start the dog showed an intense desire to hunt. He worked incessantly, trying to find moose. We continued northward along the border of Furnes until we were above the timberline. During this period Jerv reported back to his handler twice, at 7:33 A.M. and at 8:05 A.M.

"He was hunting in an unfavorable wind. Occasionally old tracks of moose were observed, but no fresh tracks were seen.

"From the Furnes district we hiked along the timberline in the general direction of Aamodt about 2700 feet above sea level. Jerv searched the territory very well.

"Approximately in the middle of our field trial course, we met another field party of four men and two dogs. Half of them joined us. At 10 A.M. Jerv was called in and leashed. When he was turned loose again 23 minutes later, he did not follow the other dog, but started promptly searching for moose tracks.

"At 10:40 A.M. he finally found what he was after; and then the fun started. The stand (*Losen*) was located in a small valley near Kvernbekken, south of Raufjellet. Jerv held the moose at bay until 11:19 A.M. We all were nearby then, but the underbrush was so dense that we could see only the moose's hindquarters. Soon the moose broke into a run, going south toward the river. Jerv followed, trying all the while to stop him and to hold him. The dog was always close behind the moose, which according to his tracks was a young animal, possibly one or two years old. Around us the country was hilly with dense woods, which made it difficult to hear. We stood quiet, lisitening, until 12:30 P.M. I couldn't say for certain that it was Jerv's voice that I heard at 12:28 P.M.

"Then we took a lunch-break, at the same time looking and listening for Jerv. Finally at 13:37 P.M. he came in, wet and grimy with swamp muck in his hair. Although he seemed tired, he alertly sniffed the air from the southwest.

"At 15:03 P.M., we turned him loose. The terrain was heavy with marsh and underbrush. He continued his search all afternoon. At from ten to twenty-five minute intervals he reported back and then was off again. But he failed to find any fresh tracks and was called in at 18 P.M.

"SUMMARY: The whole day Jerv showed an earnest desire to hunt and maintained good contact with his handler. He started out easily and controlled well when he held the moose. He had a good loud voice. With more practice this dog will show even better results. I recommend Jerv for First Prize."

(Signed) *Sigurd Hole.*

198

19

Hunting Deer with Norwegian Elkhound

By Cecil L. Graf, Chico, California

To understand how we use Elkhounds to hunt deer in California, you must first know the terrain in which we hunt deer. The area is primarily ridges and canyons, and the ground is covered with a dense growth of brush which makes a good hiding place for deer. We usually station part of our hunting party on rocky out crops while the other men and the Elkhounds drive the deer through the brush to the waiting hunters.

I do not let the Elkhounds have free run of the mountains, but have instead taught them to hunt within a hundred yard range (or less) of me. This is to keep the dogs from jumping deer too far away, where the animal is out of shooting range. If the deer start to run, the hunters on the rocky points will be able to get a shot at them, as will the hunters doing the driving through the brush.

On this particular day, everything went as planned. The Elkhounds jumped a very nice deer, a three-point buck. (Here in the West we count only one side of the antlers. By Eastern count, this would have been six points.) The deer evaded all of us in the drive, but ran into a clearing about 200 yards away from my brother stationed on a point. Although the shot was a poor one, he quickly fired at the fleeing deer.

By the time we reached the spot where the deer had last been seen, there was no sign of it. I started to check for spots of blood and hoof prints in an effort to decide whether or not the deer had been wounded.

The Elkhounds were indifferent to the whole affair and showed little excitement. I presumed the dogs were not going to help us, so we all started off to try and trail the deer. The Elkhounds trotted off ahead, staying about 25 feet ahead of me, sniffing and checking the ground as they went. Finally, I decided they knew what they were doing and just followed them.

They worked cautiously, never moving out of sight of me, or if they did, they would wait until I had a chance to catch up with them. This went on for an hour until the Elkhounds came to a clearing where physical evidence showed some disturbance had taken place. There were bits of hair, skin and scuff marks all over the area. The dogs very carefully sniffed every inch of the ground.

At this point my brother arrived, and we decided that probably a coyote had killed a young fawn and eaten most of it. It looked as if our wounded deer had walked through this area, thus confusing our dogs.

The country was getting extremely rough and brushy at this point, so we decided to spread out our hunting party before continuing the drive. I started off with the dogs and hadn't gone far when I saw Tosti starting to run with his tail wagging back and forth in excitement. He dashed ahead of me out of sight. I quickly ran to the top of a ridge where I could get a better overall view of the country. The sight before me made for one of the most interesting experiences I have had with my Elkhounds.

Tosti had found the wounded deer, which was still able to move with some speed. Instead of chasing the deer, Tosti ran ahead of him, turning him away from the brushy canyon toward which he was headed. The deer would charge the Elkhound, defying Tosti to try and keep him from entering the canyon and safety. As long as the deer had his antlers and head down, Tosti would stay his distance, but as soon as the deer would raise his head to run, Tosti would move in and lunge at his legs. The two dogs continued to circle and move in on the deer whenever they thought it was safe. Finally, both dogs moved back and I managed to get a shot at the wounded deer. After the shot, the dogs moved in on the deer very cautiously until they were sure he was dead.

I'll always wonder if Tosti really knew what he was doing when

Ch. Ravenstone Tosti of Torden,
owned by Cecil L. Graf.

he kept the deer from entering the canyon where it would have been impossible to find him, or was it just a chance happening? I believe this dog-deer hunting episode is hard to equal, regardless of breed.

My wife started the Elkhound "binge" ten years ago when she bought a two-months-old bitch to replace my German Shorthaired Pointer, the best deer dog a man could ever hope to own. Needless to say, I was skeptical about trying a different breed of hunting dog, and as a result I was very critical of our Elkhound. After several hunting trips, I became a firm believer in them as hunters. I especially like the quiet way they hunt in our brushy country. A dog that bays or barks is a detriment here because their noise chases the deer out of shooting range.

Each hunter must develop his dog to fit his individual needs, and this is what I have done with my Elkhounds. I have never kept my dogs on a leash for this would be impractical in the thick brush and undergrowth. I *do* train the Elkhounds to be quick on the recall before I take them hunting. Other than this, there is little training except to hunt a young pup with an older, experienced dog.

201

"Our Lady," registered Norwegian Elkhound, retrieving cock pheasant. Bred and owned by E. B. Kulbeck.

20

Hunting Pheasants with Norwegian Elkhounds

By Sue Ann Erickson

SINCE some of our Norwegian Elkhounds were sold to bear or mountain-lion hunters, and work very well, my husband Arv was wondering how the Elkhound would do on upland game-birds like pheasants. Well, there was one way to find out, so we took Ch. Gyda to the field on her first pheasant hunting experience—a Norwegian Elkhound as a bird dog.

Gyda started to cover the ground back and forth in front of us, about 20 to 30 feet out. She checked on us constantly and with no command would move in front of us again if we changed direction. We took her to all of our ideal spots with no result. As we were about to start on a field of standing corn, a couple of hunters emerged with a pair of "bird dogs" and assured us it was a waste of effort. While we stood there wondering where to go next, Gyda charged into the "waste of effort" and flushed a beauty. Arv shot the bird and Gyda was there when the bird hit the ground. She was very pleased with herself.

The next cornfield was larger and as we went through, Arv tried to get the dog to hunt out farther, and ignore what he thought was a gopher in the grass. Suddenly the dog gave a lunge and a pheasant exploded not five feet from him. Arv was so startled he missed the shot. Gyda went tearing off along the line of flight but the bird didn't fall. She looked at the bird disappearing and looked at Arv, with an attitude that seemed to say, "How could you miss the easy shots?"

We thought we had to teach her to hunt, and it took us quite a while to learn it was the other way around. Gyda would go right past places we thought were ideal spots for birds, and when we would call her back to work them she would casually come along. We never found a bird there. Since she limited herself to a small area in front of us, I am sure we missed birds by not following her. Proof of this came when we stopped to lunch on a hillside after a futile morning of hunting. Knowing we were going to stay put at last, she rushed down the hill to a swamp and flushed two pheasants, moved over a bit and sent up another one.

Her nephew, Chris, loved to hunt. He was 11-months-old when we first took him hunting. It was November with a strong north wind blowing sleet, and freezing temperatures. Arv and I were on either side of a creek and Chris was wading down the middle when he ran up the bank and flushed a bird. He was wild about his dead bird and nosed it over and over in the car while we drove to another field. Along the way we spotted another bird and stopped, letting the dog out to hunt with us. The bird vanished so we looked around for the dog. He was still back at the car running wildly around it trying to get in the car to his bird. We had to put the lead on him to go to the last field. Getting a scent he dashed ahead and sent up another bird. This seemed to convince him that the world was full of them, waiting to be found. He then worked the whole field from side to side, but always within range and sent up 17 in two hours. We were too stiff with cold to shoot at most, but Chris didn't care—he was in a world of his own.

When a dog can live with a cockatoo, white rats and a cat, be the companion of a two-year-old with a doll that needs rides, play ball with the boys, be the pride of the neighborhood kids because "that big dog likes me," chase rabbits on summer walks and still know that those five weekends in October and November mean pheasants only—well that's intelligence. If anyone asked me what group Elkhounds were in, I'd say they were in a class by themselves.

Mrs. E. B. Kulbeck, of Envilla Ranch, Havre, Montana, with three Norwegian Elkhounds and one day's catch of four bobcats.

Raccoon hunting with Elkhounds.

A remarkable photo of Conrad av Coulee, a 6-month-old puppy, with a bobcat at bay. Owned by Mrs. Dean Pugh.

21

Hunting Badgers with Norwegian Elkhounds

By Reidar Strömme

ONE is led to believe that each breed of dogs has its own use. And it is assumed that such was originally the case. But we have now advanced to the point where we can train any dog to do just about what we want him to do.

When one is to train a dog to hunt, he naturally chooses the breed most suitable for the purpose. Personally, I have hunted moose for twenty years. During the war when carrying guns was prohibited and moose hunting necessarily was out of the question, we learned that the Elkhound was very good at hunting the badger.

Instead of a gun, we carried a wooden cudgel as a weapon to dispatch the quarry with a blow on the forehead. It is a tense moment when advancing toward this ferocious antagonist. If something was to go wrong and the badger had an opportunity to use his long fangs on the hunter, then the man could just as well go home, that is if he was able to walk. Badger hunting was done at night, and it was against the regulations to use bright lights. Sometimes we used lights anyway.

The badger, which belongs to the marsupials, is widely distributed over Norway. The normal weight of a full grown male is approximately 17 kilograms (38 pounds) when he is ready to hibernate. The largest badger I know of weighed not less than 22 kilograms (49 pounds).

Living in underbrush near swampy channels and ditches, this animal hunts at night and returns to his den during the day. Very seldom is he out in the daytime. When that happens the badger is probably sick or has been routed. He feeds on roots, night crawlers and small animals, and steals eggs from nests. In the fall when the oats are ripe, they are his chief diet. He does not like other grains. It is in the fall in the oat fields that he is easy to hunt, because then he is enjoying an abundance of good living. One can see his flat pressed, 25 cm. wide tail through the oats. If the grain is lodged, that is where he goes. But if the grain is standing, he gathers it like a bundle and tears off the kernels. It is not unusual to find 2 or 3 kilograms (4 to 6 pounds) of oats in a badger's stomach. He generally has two dens, one for summer and another for winter. It also happens that he will share his lair with a fox, in which case you can easily discern which part is used by the fox and which by the badger. The latter, which is clean and tidy, is divided into food storage and toilet space.

The badger moves silently when afield on his short legs, but he has a terrible snarl when he is on defense or scared, somewhat between the sounds of the bear and of the pig.

Badger meat tastes something like veal or pork. Around the badger's body there is a layer of fat up to two inches thick, which he consumes during hibernation. Bounties vary from 15 to 40 crowns in various parts of the country. As there is no closed season, an excellent opportunity is presented to train Elkhounds all the year around. The Elkhounds that hunt badgers are usually in superior condition when the moose hunting season arrives.

Badger hunting with Elkhounds is quite similar to moose hunting. The only difference is that the dogs trail a little more and do not rely so much on body scent. One must be familiar with the ways of the badger and where to find him. The dog is mute until close in and then he begins a regular *stalos* (holding at bay). If the baying starts in an oat field, the badger attacks and then tries to seek refuge on a large stone, stump, or tree if he cannot reach his den.

During the badger's flight, the Elkhound will attempt to stop him by biting his rear quarters and by tossing him around, for the badger's speed is not such that he can outrun the dog. Then a

Hunting the badger. Glenna's Paal and Sorvangens Kjekk, marked with S on his side. (Dogs are marked with letters on outer coat until shedding, because collars are not used.)

different baying indicates that they are on the run (*drevlos*). If the quarry reaches his stronghold, he assumes a position with his back against a tree, stone, or whatever else is suitable. And he starts a new attack, growling and snarling all the while. The dogs continue the *stalos* just like when holding the moose at bay. Meanwhile the hunter moves cautiously toward the fighters; if far away, he must proceed rapidly. Sometimes it is desirable to allow the dog a chance to work out with the badger.

Firearms are not used until one gets close in. Then one uses a blinding light pointed directly at the badger, which will seem to be completely paralyzed. Next one advances as close as possible, to within one or one and one-half meters, continually shining the light and watching the dog, so that he does not get in front of the gun and so that he does not bite the badger, which then might be disturbed and dangerous. One should lay the revolver alongside the flashlight, unlock the safety, and then calmly and collectedly fire.

209

The bullet must hit a certain part of the forehead the size of a dime or the shot will not be vital. Only one shot should be fired, for the situation will change in the blink of an eye and a second shot would probably miss. If one waits a few seconds, he will have control of the situation again. One must also assume that the dog will attack the badger the instant the gun is fired and will try to kill him. By all means, take it easy! If there is more than one hunter in the party, the others must stay in the background. No one is permitted to shoot who has not had previous experience or who has not been trained thoroughly beforehand. The training can be accomplished at home without ammunition by aiming the gun toward a gray stone or other object. One can train in the basement where it is pitch dark. At the same time there is an opportunity to try the light beam toward certain objects. Pretend that the badger and the dog are before you in constant motion and make use of the few seconds when you imagine they are still. It is most important to get the feeling of sighting the gun, and one has to adjust his aim according to his eyes and his glasses.

When badger hunting, as before mentioned, occurs at night in autumn and close to houses in the grain field or meadow, guns of too high power should not be used. A pistol or revolver is satisfactory. I use a Colt 22 caliber long or short. The report of the gun is not disturbing and a revolver is adequate to kill a badger. We must remember that it is unusual to hunt at night (from 11 P.M. to daylight) when good folks are asleep. Those who are awakened from sleep or who are outside on an errand will believe that gangsters are staging a real hold-up and are shooting at the police dogs. One must not therefore be too surprised if the police check up as a result of someone reporting mysterious light flashes. If one has inspected the terrain during the day and has seen badger tracks in the field, it is advisable to notify the neighbors as to the night hunt and the shooting which will occur.

One goes forth an hour before darkness sets in (Norway's days are longer than in the U.S.A.) while the badger is out searching for food and while the foot scent is strong and easily followed by the dog. The main thing about this hunting, like other hunting, is that there must be good cooperation between the hunter and the dog. It is an unusual fact that the Elkhound sees better at night than in the daytime, and he can see at night as well as a cat. When a light is shone on him, his eyes reflect intensely as do those of a fox or cat. Furthermore, he will run faster on the hunt during the night; it is surprising how rapidly he can go through the brush and other obstacles. This certainly is so! We humans see very poorly in the dark, but we can become accustomed to the darkness. It is, therefore, a good idea to carry a lantern with not too bright a beam, which may be used as a walking light. The badger will not be frightened by a moving light and the dog can more easily locate the hunter. A lantern is normally used to light the way through the woods in the dark, but when one reaches the oat field, it is turned off.

During ordinary daylight hunting the rule is to watch the dog. But during night hunting the dog must keep track of the hunter. This means that the range of the Elkhound when hunting badgers will not be as wide as when hunting moose. The dog will report back, wanting the hunter to follow him. This is an important act, which cannot be appreciated enough. One can generally locate the badger and the Elkhound is sure to be there. If the dog stays with the badger night and day, then he will not be any good the rest of the hunt.

The badger hunt begins when the oats are ripe and continues until the snow comes. It will be a different training for the dog from the meager five to ten days that moose hunting has to offer.

When one has shot the badger and cannot get hold of it immediately, the dog instinctively tries to tear it to pieces. Don't scold him for that and don't worry about those few hairs lost to the barber brushes. Just let him bite. Watch when the badger drops from the shot and turn it on his back as soon as possible. Then the Elkhound can bite the chest and throat.

Even experienced hunters will find something new in badger hunting and will appreciate some advice. Remember to lock the safety on the gun as soon as the badger is dead. Chain the dog immediately. Insert the knife in its sheath after the badger's throat has been cut.

As before mentioned, a number of unusual situations may occur on a night badger hunt, and I shall close with a brief humorous story. It is about Leif Iversen, myself and Leif's Elkhound, Sikker. Sikker was not as handsome as formerly because he had too many scars and marks from the many fights with badgers. He was put to sleep at sixteen years of age, just prior to the death of his owner. He had 248 badgers and 56 moose to his credit.

We stopped the car on the field where we expected to find badgers and took Sikker to the other side of the road. He disappeared. After approximately ten minutes, his loud voice broke the stillness of the night. Between barks we heard growls and snarls (sometimes the badger will snarl like a cat). This happened in the middle of a small oat field. We could hear Sikker trying all kinds of tricks to stop the badger's flight toward a farmhouse. Those of us who had hunted with Sikker before could almost see him grasping the badger and tossing it around. Things looked bad because the badger did not stop until he reached the farmhouse, where he waged a terrific battle right under the window. Soon a light in the room was turned on and we expected to hear angry voices telling the dog to shut up. But they said nothing. The window opened and someone leaned out. We had turned off the lantern and were standing a short distance from the house. When we heard a woman's voice calling, "Yes, take him!" we knew that she understood the situation. Although it was a bit unusual, we walked to the house, introduced ourselves and put a stop to the spectacle.

A precious sight greeted us. On the steps stood a little duffer of a man in his pajamas, stooped with mouth open. He saw us coming, but was so fascinated by Sikker's encounter with the badger that he did not notice the light I shone on him. The pajamas, which seemed to be at least four sizes too big, were waving in the breeze. To hold them up, he had twisted the top of the pants as a tourniquet, which he held at his chest like a broom handle. It appeared to me that his knees were shivering. He was barefoot with big toes standing straight up. One would scarcely believe that those big feet could belong to such a small man. Hanging out the window was his wife, of opposite dimensions. Her mouth was going all the time.

Leif, who was now coming within gun range, was standing there cool and collected, aiming at the badger. The woman then burst out, "You take him, for he has killed my chickens." She could not even now keep quiet. Then my revolver was lowered and Leif peeked up at her and said, "Was that the big Minorca?"

The badger had barricaded himself under the gooseberry bush, but we finally got him. Afterward we were invited in for coffee and cake.

Mo av Hestehov, C.D., with friend. Bred by Sandra D. Speiden, and owned by Donna W. Germelman and Sandra D. Speiden.

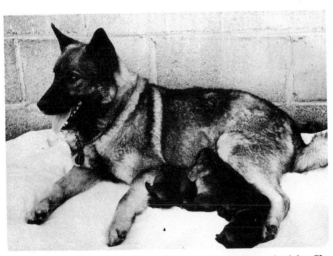

Ch. Tryg's Tulla av Hestehov, with one-day-old litter sired by Ch. Gustavus Adolphus. Bred by Mrs. Robert B. Dickson. Owned by Mrs. Wm. H. Speiden.

Roxanna's Tina (as a puppy). Owned by Edmond
C. Rabut.—Photo by Walter Chandoha.

Norwegian Elkhound puppies, owned by Florence H. Palmer,
Torvallen Kennels.

22

Do Dogs Have A Soul?
... A Testament.

SHE arrived, number three in a litter of five—big and healthy, with a little white star in the middle of her chest. Hans named her Borghild—Borgy for short. The names of all the puppies in the litter started with the letter B.

After eight weeks the mother lost interest in her offspring and it was then that Borgy assumed extra responsibility. While the rest were playing, tumbling, rolling and growling, she would sit and enjoy the spectacle. Only when little Bjorn, the smallest, was at the bottom of the pile and crying did Borgy interfere. Without being rough, she would push and pull to reach Bjorn. When he was free he would run to a corner of the yard and stand there, afraid and sulking. Borgy would follow, playing games to comfort him.

Her favorite pasttime was to sit in the back seat of the old car—she knew that if the car went, she would go along. Sometimes when young boys would draw alongside the car at a stop sign, they would annoy her by pretending to bark. She would give them an arrogant look, then turn away and sit like a queen with a world of poise.

One summer day Hans stopped in town for afternoon coffee with friends. On a neighbor's lawn, a 2-year-old boy was playing. The babysitter closed the book she had been reading and went across the street to her home. Apparently she had forgotten all about the boy. Soon the baby started after her, creeping across the sidewalk and

Ch. Borghild av Runefjell, bred and owned by Olav Wallo.

tumbling over the curb between two parked cars. He was starting to cross the busy street when Borgy got hold of the seat of his pants and slowly pulled him back across the curbing, over the sidewalk and onto the lawn. The boy seemed determined to cross the street, but each time that he tried to do so, Borgy was in front of him, pushing him back. She interested him by tossing his toys up in the air and catching them, so that he forgot all about the babysitter. Later, when the babysitter returned, she was overjoyed to find the lad safe under Borgy's faithful protection.

In another instance, a young boy disappeared from his lake home. It was in a small settlement with only a few houses surrounded by hills, woods, sloughs and lakes. By evening all of the neighbors were searching for the missing boy, and the next morning airplanes, dogs and hundreds of people had joined the search. Every square foot of ground was covered, but no trace of him was found. In the late afternoon of the second day Hans took Borgy out. Although she had no experience in tracking, he knew she would find the boy if he had crawled into some culvert or into a fox den, because she loved children. It was amazing how many things Borgy retrieved from these places—shoes, stockings and even a woman's purse with some money in it. But there was no trace of the boy.

The sun was setting when Hans decided to go home. As he walked across the meadow he looked around for Borgy. Where was she? He called and called, but no Borgy. She surely was slow. Hans turned around and started walking back across the meadow to find her. At last she came bounding over the ridge from a slough, dripping wet and muddy, but so happy. She wanted him to follow her back to the slough, but he insisted that it was time to go home. Convincing her was not easy for she did not go willingly. When they reached the house Hans learned that the boy's body had been found in the slough with one of the arms sticking out of the water. Apparently Borgy had pulled the lad ashore.

The first hard frost of November brought ice to the brooks and lakes. It was then that Tor, a two-month old puppy, tumbled over the bank, through the ice and into the brook—screaming all the while. He was trying to swim but the current swept him under the ice. Hearing the scream, Borgy came running. She spotted the hole in the ice, and followed along the bank to open water. As Tor came drifting with the current, Borgy jumped into the stream, seized the helpless puppy by the nape of the neck and dragged him to a sandbed. Tor scrambled to shore where he sat down shivering—but not for long, because Borgy nipped at her rear quarters. Although the cold, wet pup stopped frequently to upcheck the water he had swallowed, he was kept moving by his persistent rescuer. On the way home Hans put Tor under his coat to keep him warm.

Then there was that Christmas with the deep snow and below zero weather. Hans was driving to the mailbox for the Sunday paper with Borgy when he noticed a small animal emerge from the woods and dive into a culvert under the road. Peering into the long, narrow pipe, all Hans could see was a pair of eyes gleaming in the dark. With the aid of a flashlight, he discovered a small puppy, frightened and cold, too scared to move. Considerable persuasion was required on the part of Borgy before the little fellow would come out of the culvert. He was one of those mixed breeds, so often abandoned along the country roads by heartless city dwellers. He was all skin and bones and nearly blind. Hans took him home where Borgy insisted on caring for him. The puppy tagged along wherever she went.

But this did not continue long, because his eyes grew weaker day by day. The veterinarian said that he would soon be totally blind and that it would be advisable to put him to sleep. On his last ride to the veterinarian he was very frightened, climbing behind Borgy in the back seat of the car. When Hans returned from the hospital empty-handed, Borgy was waiting on the front seat, seeming to know that the little blind thing no longer needed her protection.

The next day the veterinarian reported the result of the autopsy. The puppy had had a contagious ailment, which had destroyed his liver. It was recommended that Hans have all his dogs that had been in contact with the puppy checked for the disease.

Borgy was checked, but it was too early for diagnosis. Later her stomach started swelling. She was a victim of the dread disease.

Spring brought the warm sun and the south wind. The daily hike was anticipated by all of Hans' Elghunds. As soon as the door opened they burst forth, bounding over the trail along the steep hill through the woods, down to the fragrant fields and lush lowlands. What a wonderful time, smelling, digging and chasing! In the corner by the railroad track where the underbrush grew tall and thick, two deer had their hideaway—a sombre doe and a magnificent buck. The latter waited until the dogs approached the corner, then leaped into view and swung in front of them with long, graceful strides. With no effort he jumped the 20-foot-wide creek and skipped through the high grass meadow, a silhouette of beauty in a fascinating performance. On top of the hill he stood with head high and his lofty crown appeared as a shadow on the blue horizon. By then the dogs had given up the chase.

For Borgy, those hikes were like a tonic, but as time passed it became more difficult for her to make the trip. Her appetite was not good; she lived almost solely on bread and honey balls dipped in a little fat, which Hans pushed down her throat.

Most remarkable were her eyes—beautiful, deep and dark like a small lake in the deep woods where the trees mirror themselves in clear water. On some evenings while she was sitting on the bench waiting for her supper, a strange look would appear in her eyes, revealing an almost hopeless struggle against a thing she could not understand. But she must eat her food. She would nuzzle her head under Hans' arm and keep it there until he had assured her that all was going to be well. After he patted her head, stroked her ears and promised her that she would go hunting again, her head emerged from under his arm with tears running down her cheeks and she had a look of hopeful courage. When he had dried her tears the tightly-curled tail wagged again and the honey balls slid down her throat in a hurry.

As time passed she was no longer able to take the evening hike with the other dogs. She was tied to a tree at the top of the hill. As the others passed by on the return from their romp, she would smell each one. If they had happened to contact a gopher or other animal on the way, she would wag her tail in great delight.

Then came the evening that Hans had dreaded so much, knowing that it would come sooner or later. Borgy refused to eat or to be cheered up. When the Elghunds returned from their daily hike, she showed no interest and her eyes seemed to reflect the hopeless struggle, a glance at the heart's sorrowful depths. She knew that she would not run again.

May came and Hans had mowed the first fresh green grass of the lawn. He and Borgy were sitting on the newly mown hill-top by the big oak from which they had so often enjoyed the sweeping view of the lowlands—the verdant meadows, the creek like a silver ribbon in an emerald setting, the peaceful lake with its shadows and the woods recently dressed in their springtime garb. Borgy was breathing hard, her faithful heart labored, it was near the end. As Hans was stroking the beautiful head, so many things—memories from Borgy's life—rolled by. Why should it happen to her?

After a while she walked over for a drink of water, then stumbled back, and settled in Hans' lap. She was breathing lighter now—a couple of sighs—then no more—everything still—her struggle was over.

The sun was setting. Its golden sheen flickered like a brilliant mist over the treetops. A light blue haze veiled the landscape. A meadowlark's clear song floated up from the meadow. A gust of air rustled leaves on the big oak. Was it the night wind softly whispering in the springtime leaves or was it Borgy's soul on golden wings in soaring flight toward the Great Unknown?

Ch. Just Torvald That's All, U.D., the first Norwegian Elkhound champion to also win a Utility degree in Obedience. Owned and trained by Louis H. and Kathleen Prince.

23

Safeguarding the Norwegian Elkhound

By Karen Elvin

ANYONE who selects a Norwegian Elkhound as a personal and family companion must come to realize that the breed is what it is primarily because of the thousands of years of natural selection that have cultivated in it the qualities that make it so satisfactory a hunter, family guardian, and protector. Neither fashion nor single purpose has distorted the physical and mental attributes of the Elkhound. He is a dog of moderation and general usefulness, best suited of all domestic breeds to perform the variety of tasks required in his long and close association with the human race. In order to honor and protect the breed, those who have taken it upon themselves to supervise its propagation should seek to preserve the best of what Nature herself has developed over the centuries.

However, Nature is not without the capacity to make mistakes. In Elkhounds, as in all other breeds, conditions exist which, if allowed to persist through thoughtless or misguided breeding practises engineered by man, endanger both the basic soundness and breed type of the Elkhound. Left to herself, Nature would eliminate individuals who do not meet her standards of performance. Man interferes, with the result that serious problems are often genetically spread throughout the breeding population by those unaware, or if aware—choosing to hide and ignore their presence.

Problems which breeders of Elkhounds must recognize and eliminate include: hip dysplasia; entropion; poor temperament; progressive retinal atrophy; monorchidism; jaw deformities; predisposition to skin disease; reproductive abnormalities and other difficulties that can render dogs unsound for utilitarian purposes, and can cause much heartbreak when affecting a family pet. Animals displaying these difficulties should not be used for breeding. Many times such dogs can compensate for their difficulties and live out their lives as family companions, but under no circumstances should these mistakes of nature be propagated.

The best defense against the widespread dissemination of these genetic mistakes is information. The Breeders Division of the Norwegian Elkhound Association of Minnesota in 1960 began an effort to provide an agency which would stand for integrity and quality in the breeding of Elkhounds. To do this, its members have attempted to collect and pool information about the genetic makeup of the breed, so that breeders can inform themselves of problems and potential improvements that each planned mating may possibly produce.

Hip dysplasia has been the subject of much discussion in dog journals in recent years and many Elkhound breeders are aware that it exists as a threat to the soundness of their breed. While researchers are not in agreement as to its mode of inheritance, without exception they have concluded that the incidence of malformed crippled hip joints can be substantially reduced by breeding only animals whose pelvic radiographs show no evidence of dysplasia.

The Minnesota Breeders Division members have X-rayed breeding stock for several years in hope of building pedigree depth behind their dogs and working for the reduction of the incidence of dysplasia in Elkhounds.

Many national breed clubs and the NEAM Breeders Division support the work and utilize the facilities of the Orthopedic Foundation for Animals, Inc., Columbia, Mo. 65201, an institution founded to study musculoskeletal diseases in animals and to aid breeders wishing to submit radiographs for interpretation by a panel of veterinary radiologists. Since the Norwegian Elkhound Association of America in 1967 established a committee to study the problem of hip dysplasia in Elkhounds, it is hoped that the NEAA will soon support the OFA as have other national breed clubs including the German Shepherd Dog, English Springer Spaniel, Old English Sheepdog, Samoyed, Standard and Giant Schnauzers, Labrador Retriever, German Shorthaired Pointer and other clubs; and that they will encourage breeder-members to use only animals certified by the OFA to be free from dysplasia in their breeding programs.

Another grave problem for the breed is progressive retinal atrophy, which causes blindness in affected animals. Test breedings with Irish Setters and Poodles, breeds which also contain in their genetic makeup the factors which produce this crippling fault, have shown it to be a simple Mendelian recessive factor. Two unaffected parents carrying the recessive gene for PRA can produce offspring afflicted with the disease. If used for breeding, animals that are affected with PRA will produce offspring which are carriers of the recessive factor when mated to normal animals not carrying the recessive gene. Affected animals mated to carriers may produce both carriers and affected animals. If, for experimental purpose, two affected animals are mated, their offspring would all be affected. Some test matings in Elkhounds have indicated that the mode of inheritance for this breed may be affected by other factors such as stress from disease. Nonetheless, it is certainly inadvisable to breed an animal with PRA or one which has produced affected offspring.

Another factor making the task of the breeder doubly hard is the fact that often PRA is not detectable until a dog is three years of age or older. Owners of dogs that are kept as pets may not detect that their dog has lost part or all of its sight and some cases may never be brought to the attention of the breeder. Concerned breeders should do their utmost to obtain knowledge of the ancestors, siblings, and offspring of their breeding animals, and should have their breeding stock examined in an effort to eliminate PRA.

Next to these physical anomolies, one of the greatest threats to the breed fostered by indiscriminate breeding practises is the perversion of an Elkhound's most indelible feature, his temperament. An Elkhound that is not bold and energetic is a deviation from the standard, just as much as is one that is brown or has a straight tail. Shy, nervous, vicious, or stupid Elkhounds should never be used for breeding. While environment influences, heredity determines. The degree of stability of temperament in the typical Elkhound is his

Erik Marken and Runefjell Torvald.

distinguishing feature. Let it not be lost in preference to physical features dictated by fashion.

Other factors such as undershot jaws, entropion, lop ears, and off colors may be features which do not seriously incapacitate a dog, yet they are not true Elkhound characteristics. Dogs possessing them should be withheld from breeding, or the characteristics may become genetically widespread in the breed and very difficult to eradicate.

The best defense against the proliferation of such problems is information. Breeders organized to pool their information frankly, with the ultimate best interests of the breed in mind, can do much to preserve and improve an already utilitarian breed, designed by Nature to serve and survive.

Publisher's Note: At press-time we are advised that a most active program encouraging and recording X-raying of dogs has been undertaken by a committee of the parent Norwegian Elkhound Association of America, headed by Henry M. Glasgow, and it is receiving excellent cooperation from the membership.

24

Training and Simple Obedience

EVERY DOG that is mentally and physically sound can be taught good manners and simple obedience by any normal man, woman, or child over eight years old.

Certain requirements must be met by the dog, trainer and the environment if the training is to be enjoyable and effective. The dog must be rested and calm. The trainer must be rested, calm, gentle, firm, patient and persistent. The training site should be dry, comfortable and, except for certain exercises, devoid of distractions.

Proper techniques can achieve quick and sure results. Always use short, strong words for commands and always use the *same* word or words for the same command. Speak with authority; never scream or yell. Teach one command or exercise at a time and make sure the dog understands it and performs it perfectly before you proceed to the next step. Demand the dog's undivided attention; if he wavers or wanders, speak his name or pat him smartly or jerk his leash. Use pats and praise plentifully; avoid tidbit training if at all possible because tidbits may not always be available in an emergency and the dog will learn better without them. Keep lessons short; when the dog begins to show boredom, stop and do not resume in less than two hours. One or two ten-minute lessons a day should be ample, especially for a young puppy. Dogs have their good and bad days; if your well dog seems unduly lazy, tired, bored or off-color, put off the lesson until tomorrow. Try to make lessons a joy, a happy time both for you and the dog, but do demand and get the desired action. Whenever correction or punishment is needed, use ways and devices that the dog does not connect with you; some of these means are given in the following instructions. Use painful punishment only as a last resort.

"NO!"

The most useful and easily understood command is "NO!" spoken in a sharp, disapproving tone and accompanied with a shaking finger. At first, speak the dog's name following with "NO!" until the meaning of the word—your displeasure—is clear.

"COME!"

Indoors or out, let the dog go ten or more feet away from you. Speak his name following at once with "COME!" Crouch, clap your hands, pick up a stick, throw a ball up and catch it, or create any other diversion which will lure the dog to you. When he comes, praise and pat effusively. As with all commands and exercises repeat the lesson, until the dog *always* comes to you.

THE FIRST NIGHTS

Puppies left alone will bark, moan and whine. If your dog is not to have the run of the house, put him in a room where he can do the least damage. Give him a Nylabone and a strip of beef hide (both available in supermarkets or pet shops and excellent as teething pacifiers). A very young puppy may appreciate a loud-ticking clock which, some dog trainers say, simulates the heart-beat of his former litter mates. Beyond providing these diversions, grit your teeth and steel your heart. If in pity you go to the howling puppy, he will howl every time you leave him. Suffer one night, two nights or possibly three, and you'll have it made.

The greatest boon to dog training and management is the wooden or wire crate. Any two-handed man can make a ⅜″ plywood crate. It needs only four sides, a top, a bottom, a door on hinges and with a strong hasp, and a fitting burlap bag stuffed with shredded newspaper, cedar shavings or 2″ foam rubber. Feed dealers or seed stores should give you burlap bags; be sure to wash them thoroughly to remove any chemical or allergy-causing material. The crate should be as long, as high and three times as wide as the dog will be full grown. The crate will become as much a sanctuary to your dog as a cave was to his prehistoric ancestor; it will also help immeasurably in housebreaking.

HOUSEBREAKING

The secret to housebreaking a healthy normal dog is simple: take him out every hour if he is from two to six months old when you get him; or the first thing in the morning, immediately after every meal, and the last thing at night if he is over six months.

For very young puppies, the paper break is indicated. Lay eight or ten layers of newspapers in a room corner most remote from the puppy's bed. By four months of age or after two weeks in a new home if older, a healthy puppy should not need the paper *IF* it is exercised outdoors often and *IF* no liquid (including milk) is given after 5 P.M. and *IF* it is taken out not earlier than 10 P.M. at night and not later than 7 A.M. the next morning.

When the dog does what it should when and where it should, praise, praise and praise some more. Be patient outdoors: keep the dog out until action occurs. Take the dog to the same general area always; its own traces and those of other dogs thus drawn to the spot will help to inspire the desired action.

In extreme cases where frequent exercising outdoors fails, try to catch the dog in the act and throw a chain or a closed tin can with pebbles in it near the dog but not on him; say "NO!" loudly as the chain or can lands. In the most extreme case, a full 30-second spanking with a light strap may be indicated but be sure you catch the miscreant *in the act*. Dog memories are short.

Remember the crate discussed under "THE FIRST NIGHTS." If you give the dog a fair chance, he will NOT soil his crate.

Do not rub his nose in "it." Dogs have dignity and pride. It is permissible to lead him to his error as soon as he commits it and to remonstrate forcefully with "NO!"

COLLAR AND LEASH TRAINING

Put on a collar tight enough not to slip over the head. Leave it on for lengthening periods from a few minutes to a few hours over several days. A flat collar for shorthaired breeds; a round or rolled collar for longhairs. For collar breaking, do NOT use a choke collar; it may catch on a branch or other jutting object and strangle the dog.

After a few days' lessons with the collar, attach a heavy cord or rope to it without a loop or knot at the end (to avoid snagging or catching on a stump or other object). Allow the dog to run free with collar and cord attached a few moments at a time for several days. Do not allow dog to chew cord!

When the dog appears to be accustomed to the free-riding cord, pick up end of the cord, loop it around your hand and take your dog for a walk (not the other way around!). DON'T STOP WALKING if the dog pulls, balks or screams bloody murder. Keep going and make encouraging noises. If dog leaps ahead of you, turn sharply left or right whichever is *away* from dog's direction—AND KEEP MOVING! The biggest mistake in leash training is stopping when the dog stops, or going the way the dog goes when the dog goes wrong. You're the leader; make the dog aware of it. This is one lesson you should continue until the dog realizes who is boss. If the dog gets the upper leg now, you will find it difficult to resume your rightful position as master. Brutality, no; firmness, yes!

If the dog pulls ahead, jerk the cord—or by now, the leash—backward. Do not pull. Jerk or snap the leash only!

JUMPING ON PEOPLE

Nip this annoying habit at once by bumping the dog with your knee on his chest or stepping with authority on his rear feet. A sharp "NO!" at the same time helps. Don't permit this action when you're in your work clothes and ban it only when dressed in glad rags. The dog is not Beau Brummel, and it is cruel to expect him to distinguish between denim and silk.

THE "PROBLEM" DOG

The following corrections are indicated when softer methods fail. Remember that it's better to rehabilitate than to destroy.

Biting. For the puppy habit of mouthing or teething on the owner's hand, a sharp rap with a folded newspaper on the nose, or snapping the middle finger off the thumb against the dog's nose, will usually discourage nibbling tactics. For the biter that means it, truly drastic corrections may be preferable to destroying the dog. If your dog is approaching one year of age and is biting in earnest, take him to a professional dog trainer and don't quibble with his methods unless you would rather see the dog dead.

Chewing. For teething puppies, provide a Nylabone (trade mark) and beef hide strips (see "THE FIRST NIGHTS" above). Every time the puppy attacks a chair, a rug, your hand, or any other chewable object, snap your finger or rap a newspaper on his nose, or throw the chain or a covered pebble-laden tin can near him, say "NO!" and hand him the bone or beef hide. If he persists, put him in his crate with the bone and hide. For incorrigible chewers, check diet for deficiencies first. William Koehler, trainer of many movie dogs including *The Thin Man's* Asta, recommends in his book, *The Koehler Method of Dog Training,* that the chewed object or part of it be taped crosswise in the dog's mouth until he develops a hearty distaste for it.

Digging. While he is in the act, throw the chain or noisy tin can and call out "NO!" For the real delinquent Koehler recommends filling the dug hole with water, forcing the dog's nose into it until the dog thinks he's drowning—and he'll never dig again. Drastic perhaps, but better than the bullet from an angry neighbor's gun, or a surreptitious poisoning.

The Runaway. If your dog wanders while walking with you, throw the chain or tin can and call "COME!" to him. If he persists, have a friend or neighbor cooperate in chasing him home. A very long line, perhaps 25 feet or more, can be effective if you permit the dog to run its length and then snap it sharply to remind him not to get too far from you.

Car Chasing. Your dog will certainly live longer if you make him car-wise; in fact, deathly afraid of anything on wheels. Ask a friend or neighbor to drive you in *his* car. Lie below the windows and as your dog chases the car throw the chain or tin can while your neighbor or friend says "GO HOME!" sharply. Another method is to shoot a water pistol filled with highly diluted ammonia at the dog. If your dog runs after children on bicycles, the latter device is especially effective but may turn the dog against children.

The Possessive Dog. If a dog displays overly protective habits, berate him in no uncertain terms. The chain, the noisy can, the rolled newspaper, or light strap sharply applied, may convince him that, while he loves you, there's no percentage in overdoing it.

The Cat Chaser. Again, the chain, the can, the newspaper, the strap—or the cat's claws if all else fails, but only as the last resort.

The Defiant, or Revengeful, Wetter. Some dogs seem to resent being left alone. Some are jealous when their owners play with another dog or animal. Get a friend or neighbor in this case to heave the chain or noisy tin can when the dog relieves himself in sheer spite.

For other canine delinquencies, you will find *The Koehler Method of Dog Training* effective. William Koehler's techniques have been certified as extremely successful by directors of motion pictures featuring dogs and by officers of dog obedience clubs.

OBEDIENCE EXERCISES

A well-mannered dog saves its owner money, embarrassment and possible heartbreak. The destruction of property by canine delinquents, avoidable accidents to dogs and children, and other unnecessary disadvantages to dog ownership can be eliminated by simple obedience training. The elementary exercises of heeling, sitting, staying and lying down can keep the dog out of trouble in most situations.

The only tools needed for basic obedience training are a slip collar made of chain link, leather or nylon and a strong six-foot leather leash with a good spring snap. Reviewing the requirements and basic techniques given earlier, let's proceed with the dog's schooling.

Heeling. Keep your dog on your left side, with the leash in your left hand. Start straight ahead in a brisk walk. If your dog pulls ahead, jerk (do not pull) the leash and say "Heel" firmly. If the dog persists in pulling ahead, stop, turn right or left and go on for several yards, saying "Heel" each time you change direction.

If your dog balks, fix leash *under* his throat and coax him forward by repeating his name and tapping your hip.

Whatever you do, don't stop walking! If the dog jumps up or "fights" the leash, just keep moving briskly. Sooner than later he will catch on and with the repetition of "Heel" on every correction, you will have him trotting by your side with style and respect.

Sit. Keeping your dog on leash, hold his neck up and push his rump down while repeating "Sit." If he resists, "spank" him lightly several times on his rump. Be firm, but not cruel. Repeat this lesson often until it is learned perfectly. When the dog knows the command, test him at a distance without the leash. Return to him every time he fails to sit and repeat the exercise.

Stay. If you have properly trained your dog to "Sit," the "Stay" is simple. Take his leash off and repeat "Stay" holding your hand up, palm toward dog, and move away. If dog moves toward you, you must repeat the "sit" lesson until properly learned. After your dog "stays" while you are in sight, move out of his sight and keep repeating "Stay." Once he has learned to "stay" even while you are out of his sight, you can test him under various conditions, such as when another dog is near, a child is playing close to him, or a car appears on the road. (Warning: do not tax your dog's patience on the "stay" until he has learned the performance perfectly.)

Down.   For this lesson, keep your dog on leash. First tell him to "sit." When he has sat for a minute, place your shoe over his leash between the heel and sole. Slowly pull on the leash and repeat "Down" while you push his head down with your other hand. Do this exercise very quietly so that dog does not become excited and uncontrollable. In fact, this performance is best trained when the dog is rather quiet. Later, after the dog has learned the voice signal perfectly, you can command the "Down" with a hand signal, sweeping your hand from an upright position to a downward motion with your palm toward the dog. Be sure to say "Down" with the hand signal.

For more advanced obedience the following guides by Blanche Saunders are recommended:

The Complete Novice Obedience Course
The Complete Open Obedience Course
The Complete Utility Obedience Course (with Tracking)
Dog Training for Boys and Girls (includes simple tricks.)
All are published by Howell Book House at $3.00 each.

OBEDIENCE TRIALS

Booklets covering the rules and regulations of Obedience Trials may be obtained from The American Kennel Club, 51 Madison Avenue, New York, N.Y. 10010. In Canada, write The Canadian Kennel Club, 667 Yonge Street, Toronto, Ontario.

Both these national clubs can give you the names and locations of local and regional dog clubs that conduct training classes in obedience and run Obedience Trials in which trained dogs compete for degrees as follow: CD (Companion Dog), CDX (Companion Dog Excellent), UD (Utility Dog), TD (Tracking Dog) and UDT (Utility Dog, Tracking.)

25

Housing for Dogs

EVERY owner will have, and will have to solve, his own problems about providing his dog or dogs with quarters best suited to the dog's convenience. The special circumstances of each particular owner will determine what kind of home he will provide for his dogs. Here it is impossible to provide more than a few generalities upon the subject.

Little more need be said than that fit quarters for dogs must be secure, clean, dry, and warm. Consideration must be given to convenience in the care of kennel inmates by owners of a large number of dogs, but by the time one's activities enlarge to such proportions one will have formulated one's own concept of how best to house one's dogs. Here, advice will be predicated upon the maintenance of not more than three or four adult dogs with accommodations for an occasional litter of puppies.

First, let it be noted that dogs are not sensitive to aesthetic considerations in the place they are kept; they have no appreciation of the beauty of their surroundings. They do like soft beds of sufficient thickness to protect them from the coldness of the floors. These beds should be secluded and covered to conserve body heat. A box or crate of adequate size to permit the dog to lie full length in it will suffice. The cushion may be a burlap bag stuffed with shredded paper, *not straw, hay, or grass*. Paper is recommended, for its use will reduce the possibility of the dog's developing skin trouble.

Most dogs are allergic to fungi found on vegetative matter such as straw, hay, and grass. Wood shavings and excelsior may be used with impunity.

The kennel should be light, except for a retiring place; if sunshine is available at least part of the day, so much the better. Boxes in a shed or garage with secure wire runs to which the dogs have ready access suffice very well, are very inexpensive, and are easy to plan and to arrange. The runs should be made of wire fencing strong enough that the dogs are unable to tear it with their teeth and high enough that the dogs are unable to jump or climb over it. In-turning flanges of wire netting at the tops of the fences tend to obviate jumping. Boards, rocks, or cement buried around the fences forestall burrowing to freedom.

These pens need not be large, if the dogs are given frequent respites from their captivity and an opportunity to obtain needed exercise. However, they should be large enough to relieve them of the aspect of cages. Concrete floors for such pens are admittedly easy to keep clean and sanitary. However, they have no resilience, and the feet of dogs confined for long periods on concrete floors are prone to spread and their shoulders to loosen. A further objection to concrete is that it grows hot in the summer sunshine and is very cold in winter. If it is used for flooring at all, a low platform of wood, large enough to enable the dogs to sprawl out on it full length, should be provided in each pen.

A well drained soil is to be preferred to concrete, if it is available; but it must be dug out to the depth of three inches and renewed occasionally, if it is used. Otherwise, the accumulation of urine will make it sour and offensive. Agricultural limestone, applied monthly and liberally, will "sweeten" the soil.

Gates, hinges, latches, and other hardware must be trustworthy. The purpose of such quarters is to confine the dogs and to keep them from running at large; unless they serve such a purpose they are useless. One wants to know when one puts a dog in his kennel, the dog will be there when one returns. An improvised kennel of old chicken wire will not suffice for one never knows whether it will hold one's dogs or not.

Frequently two friendly bitches may be housed together, or a dog housed with a bitch. Unless one is sure of male friendships, it is seldom safe to house two adult male dogs together. It is better, if possible, to provide a separate kennel for each mature dog. But, if the dogs can be housed side by side with only a wire fence between them, they can have companionship without rancor. Night barking can be controlled by confining the dogs indoors or by shutting them up in their boxes.

Adult dogs require artificial heat in only the coldest of climates, if they are provided with tight boxes placed under shelter. Puppies need heat in cold weather up until weaning time, and even thereafter if they are not permitted to sleep together. Snuggled together in a tight box with shredded paper, they can withstand much cold without discomfort. All dogs in winter without artificial heat should have an increase of their rations—especially as pertains to fat content.

Whatever artificial heat is provided for dogs should be safe, foolproof, and dog-proof. Caution should be exercised that electric wiring is not exposed, that stoves cannot be tipped over, and that it is impossible for sparks from them to ignite the premises. Many fires in kennels, the results of defective heating apparatus or careless handling of it, have brought about the deaths of the inmates. It is because of them that this seemingly unnecessary warning is given.

No better place for a dog to live can be found than the home of its owner, sharing even his bed if permitted. So is the dog happiest. There is a limit, however, to the number of dogs that can be tolerated in the house. The keeper of a small kennel can be expected to alternate his favorite dogs in his own house, thus giving them a respite to confinement in a kennel. Provision must be made for a place of exercise and relief at frequent intervals for dogs kept in the house. An enclosed dooryard will serve such a purpose, or the dog may be exercised on a lead with as much benefit to the owner as to the dog.

That the quarters of the dog shall be dry is even more important than that they shall be warm. A damp, drafty kennel is the cause of much kennel disease and indisposition. It is harmless to permit a dog to go out into inclement weather of his own choice, if he is provided with a sheltered bed to which he may retire to dry himself.

By cleanness, sanitation is meant—freedom from vermin and bacteria. A little coat of dust or a degree of disorder does not discommode the dog or impair his welfare, but the best dog keepers are orderly persons. They at least do not permit bedding and old bones to accumulate in a dog's bed, and they take the trouble to spray with antiseptic or wash with soap and water their dog's house at frequent intervals. The feces in the kennel runs should be picked up and destroyed at least once, and better twice, daily. Persistent filth in kennels can be counted on as a source of illness sooner or later. This warning appears superfluous, but it isn't; the number of ailing dogs kept in dirty, unsanitary kennels is amazing. It is one of the axioms of keeping dogs that their quarters must be sanitary or disease is sure to ensue.

GOOD DOG KEEPING PRACTICES

Pride of ownership is greatly enhanced when the owner takes care to maintain his dog in the best possible condition at all times. And meticulous grooming not only will make the dog look better but also will make him feel better. As part of the regular, daily routine, the grooming of the dog will prove neither arduous nor time consuming; it will also obviate the necessity for indulging in a rigorous program designed to correct the unkempt state in which too many owners permit their dogs to appear. Certainly, spending a few minutes each day will be well worth while, for the result will be a healthier, happier, and more desirable canine companion.

THAT DOGGY ODOR

Many persons are disgusted to the point of refusal to keep a dog by what they fancy is a "doggy odor." Of course, almost everything has a characteristic odor—everyone is familiar with the smell of the rose. No one would want the dog to smell like a rose, and, conversely, the world wouldn't like it very well if the rose smelled doggy. The dog must emit a certain amount of characteristic odor or he wouldn't be a dog. That seems to be his God-given grant. However, when the odor becomes too strong and obnoxious, then it is time to look for the reason. In most cases it is the result of clogged anal glands. If this be the case, all one must do to rid the pet of his odor is to express the contents of these glands and apply to the anal region a little soap and water.

If the odor is one of putrefaction, look to his mouth for the trouble. The teeth may need scaling, or a diseased root of some one or two teeth that need to be treated may be the source of the odor. In some dogs there is a fold or a crease in the lower lip near the lower canine tooth, and this may need attention. This spot is favored by fungi that cause considerable damage to the part. The smell here is somewhat akin to the odor of human feet that have been attacked by the fungus of athlete's foot.

The odor may be coming from the coat if the dog is heavily infested with fleas or lice. Too, dogs seem to enjoy the odor of dead fish and often roll on a foul smelling fish that has been cast up on the beach. The dog with a bad case of otitis can fairly "drive you out of the room" with this peculiar odor. Obviously, the way to rid the dog of odor is to find from whence it comes and then take steps to eliminate it. Some dogs have a tendency toward excessive flatulence (gas). These animals should have a complete change of diet and with the reducing of the carbohydrate content, a teaspoon of granular charcoal should be added to each feeding.

BATHING THE DOG

There is little to say about giving a bath to a dog, except that he shall be placed in a tub of warm (not hot) water and thoroughly scrubbed. He may, like a spoiled child, object to the ordeal, but if handled gently and firmly he will submit to what he knows to be inevitable.

The water must be only tepid, so as not to shock or chill the dog. A bland, unmedicated soap is best, for such soaps do not irritate the skin or dry out the hair. Even better than soap is one of the powdered detergents marketed especially for this purpose. They rinse away better and more easily than soap and do not leave the coat gummy or sticky.

It is best to begin with the face, which should be thoroughly and briskly washed with a cloth. Care should be taken that the cleaning solvent does not get into the dog's eyes, not because of the likelihood of causing permanent harm, but because such an experience is unpleasant to the dog and prone to prejudice him against future baths. The interior of the ear canals should be thoroughly cleansed until they not only look clean but also until no unpleasant odor comes from them. The head may then be rinsed and dried before proceeding to the body. Especial attention should be given to the drying of the ears, inside and outside. Many ear infections arise from failure to dry the canals completely.

With the head bathed and the surplus water removed from that part, the body must be soaked thoroughly with water, either with a hose or by dipping the water from the bath and pouring it over the dog's back until he is totally wetted. Thereafter, the soap or detergent should be applied and rubbed until it lathers freely. A stiff brush is useful in penetrating the coat and cleansing the skin. It is not sufficient to wash only the back and sides—the belly, neck, legs, feet, and tail must all be scrubbed thoroughly.

If the dog is very dirty, it may be well to rinse him lightly and repeat the soaping process and scrub again. Thereafter, the dog must be rinsed with warm (tepid) water until all suds and soil come away. If a bath spray is available, the rinsing is an easy matter. If the dog must be rinsed in standing water, it will be needful to renew it two or three times.

When he is thoroughly rinsed, it is well to remove such surplus water as may be squeezed with the hand, after which he is enveloped with a turkish towel, lifted from the tub, and rubbed until he is dry. This will probably require two or three dry towels. In the process of drying the dog, it is well to return again and again to the interior of the ears.

THE DOG'S TEETH

The dog, like the human being, has two successive sets of teeth, the so-called milk teeth or baby teeth, which are shed and replaced later by the permanent teeth. The temporary teeth, which begin to emerge when the puppy is two and a half to three weeks of age, offer no difficulty. The full set of milk teeth (consisting usually of six incisors and two canines in each jaw, with four molars in the upper jaw and six molars in the lower jaw) is completed usually just before weaning time. Except for some obvious malformation, the milk teeth may be ignored and forgotten about.

At about the fourth month the baby teeth are shed and gradually replaced by the permanent teeth. This shedding and replacement process may consume some three or four months. This is about the most critical period of the dog's life—his adolescence. Some constitutionally vigorous dogs go through their teething easily, with no seeming awareness that the change is taking place. Others, less vigorous, may suffer from soreness of the gums, go off in flesh, and require pampering. While they are teething, puppies should be particularly protected from exposure to infectious diseases and should be fed on nutritious foods, especially meat and milk.

The permanent teeth normally consist of 42—six incisors and two canines (fangs) in each jaw, with twelve molars in the upper jaw and fourteen in the lower jaw. Occasionally the front molars fail to emerge; this deficiency is considered by most judges to be only a minor fault, if the absence is noticed at all.

Dentition is a heritable factor in the dog, and some dogs have soft, brittle and defective permanent teeth, no matter how excellent the diet and the care given them. The teeth of those dogs which are predisposed to have excellent sound ones, however, can be ruined by an inferior diet prior to and during the period of their eruption. At this time, for the teeth to develop properly, a dog must have an adequate supply of calcium phosphate and vitamin D, besides all the protein he can consume.

Often the permanent teeth emerge before the shedding of the milk teeth, in which case the dog may have parts of both sets at the same time. The milk teeth will eventually drop out, but as long as they remain they may deflect or displace the second teeth in the process of their growth. The incisors are the teeth in which a malformation may result from the late dropping of the baby teeth. When it is realized just how important a correct "bite" may be deemed in the show ring, the hazards of permitting the baby teeth to deflect the permanent set will be understood.

The baby teeth in such a case must be dislodged and removed. The roots of the baby teeth are resorbed in the gums, and the teeth can usually be extracted by firm pressure of thumb and finger, although it may be necessary to employ forceps or to take the puppy to the veterinarian.

The permanent teeth of the puppy are usually somewhat overshot, by which is meant that the upper incisors protrude over and do not play upon the lower incisors. Maturity may be trusted to remedy this apparent defect unless it is too pronounced.

An undershot mouth in a puppy, on the other hand, tends to grow worse as the dog matures. Whether or not it has been caused by the displacement of the permanent teeth by the persistence of the milk teeth, it can sometimes be remedied (or at least bettered) by frequent hard pressure of the thumb on the lower jaw, forcing the lower teeth backward to meet the upper ones. Braces on dog teeth have seldom proved efficacious, but pressure and massage are worth trying on the bad mouth of an otherwise excellent puppy.

High and persistent fevers, especially from the fourth to the ninth month, sometimes result in discolored, pitted, and defective teeth, commonly called "distemper teeth." They often result from maladies other than distemper. There is little that can be done for them. They are unpleasant to see and are subject to penalty in the show ring, but are serviceable to the dog. Distemper teeth are not in themselves heritable, but the predisposition for their development appears to be. At least, at the teething age, the offspring from distemper toothed ancestors seem to be especially prone to fevers which impair their dentition.

Older dogs, especially those fed largely upon carbohydrates, tend to accumulate more or less tartar upon their teeth. The tartar generally starts at the gum line on the molars and extends gradually to the cusp. To rectify this condition, the dog's teeth should be scaled by a veterinarian.

The cleanliness of a dog's mouth may be brought about and the formation of tartar discouraged by the scouring of the teeth with a moist cloth dipped in a mixture of equal parts of table salt and baking soda.

A large bone given the dog to chew on or play with tends to prevent tartar from forming on the teeth. If tartar is present, the chewing and gnawing on the bone will help to remove the deposit mechanically. A bone given to puppies will act as a teething ring and aid in the cutting of the permanent teeth. So will beef hide strips you can buy in pet shops.

CARE OF THE NAILS

The nails of the dog should be kept shortened and blunted right down to the quick—never into the quick. If this is not done, the toes may spread and the foot may splay into a veritable pancake. Some dogs have naturally flat feet, which they have inherited. No pretense is made that the shortening of the nails of such a foot will obviate the fault entirely and make the foot beautiful or serviceable.

It will only improve the appearance and make the best of an obvious fault. Short nails do, however, emphasize the excellence of a good foot.

Some dogs keep their nails short by digging and friction. Their nails require little attention, but it is a rare dog whose foot cannot be bettered by artificially shortening the nails.

Nail clippers are available, made especially for the purpose. After using them, the sides of the nail should be filed away as much as is possible without touching the quick. Carefully done, it causes the dog no discomfort. But, once the quick of a dog's nail has been injured, he may forever afterward resent and fight having his feet treated or even having them examined.

The obvious horn of the nail can be removed, after which the quick will recede to permit the removal of more horn the following week. This process may be kept up until the nail is as short and blunt as it can be made, after which nails will need attention only at intervals of six weeks or two months.

Some persons clip the nails right back to the toes in one fell swoop, disregarding injury to the quick and pain of the dog. The nails bleed and the dog limps for a day or two, but infection seldom develops. Such a procedure should not be undertaken without a general anesthetic. If an anesthetic is used, this forthright method does not prejudice the dog against having his feet handled.

NAIL TRIMMING ILLUSTRATED

The method here illustrated is to take a sharp file and stroke the nail downwards in the direction of the arrow, as in Figure 24, until it assumes the shape in Figure 25, the shaded portion being the part removed, a three-cornered file should then be used on the underside just missing the quick, as in Figure 26, and the operation is then complete, the dog running about quickly wears the nail to the proper shape.

COAT CARE

Skin troubles can often be checked and materially alleviated by proper grooming. Every dog is entitled to the minimum of weekly attention to coat, skin and ears; ideally, a daily stint with brush and comb is highly recommended. Frequent examination may catch skin disease in its early stages and provide a better chance for a quick cure.

The outer or "guard" hairs of a dog's coat should glint in the sunlight. There should be no mats or dead hair in the coat. Wax in the outer ear should be kept at a minimum.

It is helpful to stand the dog on a flat, rigid surface off the floor at a height convenient to the groomer. Start at the head and ears brushing briskly *with* the lay of short hair, *against* the lay of long hair at first then with it. After brushing, use a fine comb with short teeth on fine, short hair and a coarse comb with long teeth on coarse or long hair. If mats cannot be readily removed with brush or comb, use barber's thinning shears and cut into the matted area several times until mat pulls free easily. Some mats can be removed with the fingers if one has the patience to separate the hair a bit at a time.

After brushing and combing, run your palms over the dog's coat from head to tail. Natural oils in your skin will impart sheen to your dog's coat.

The ears of some dogs secrete and exude great amounts of wax. Frequent examination will determine when your dog's ears need cleaning. A thin coating of clean, clear wax is not harmful. But a heavy accumulation of dirty, dark wax needs removal by cotton pads soaked in diluted hydrogen peroxide (3% cut in half with boiled water), or alcohol or plain boiled water if wax is not too thick.

There are sprays, "dry" bath preparations and other commercial products for maintaining your dog's coat health. Test them first, and if they are successful, you may find them beneficial time-savers in managing your dog's coat.

First Aid

JOHN STEINBECK, the Nobel Prize winning author, in *Travels with Charley in Search of America* bemoans the lack of a good, comprehensive book of home dog medicine. Charley is the aged Poodle that accompanies his illustrious author-owner on a motor tour of the U.S.A.

As in human medicine, most treatment and dosing of dogs are better left in the experienced, trained hands and mind of a professional—in this case, the veterinarian. However, there are times and situations when professional aid is not immediately available and an owner's prompt action may save a life or avoid permanent injury. To this purpose, the following suggestions are given.

The First Aid Kit

For instruments keep on hand a pair of tweezers, a pair of pliers, straight scissors, a rectal thermometer, a teaspoon, a tablespoon, and swabs for cotton.

For dressings, buy a container of cotton balls, a roll of cotton and a roll of 2″ gauze. Strips of clean, old sheets may come in handy.

For medicines, stock ammonia, aspirin, brandy, 3% hydrogen peroxide, bicarbonate of soda, milk of bismuth, mineral oil, salt, tea, vaseline, kaopectate, baby oil and baby talcum powder.

Handling the Dog for Treatment

Approach any injured or sick dog calmly with reassuring voice and gentle, steady hands. If the dog is in pain, slip a gauze or sheet strip noose over its muzzle tying the ends first under the throat and then back of the neck. Make sure the dog's lips are not caught between his teeth, but make noose around muzzle *tight*.

If the dog needs to be moved, grasp the loose skin on the back of the neck with one hand and support chest with the other hand. If the dog is too large to move in this manner, slide him on a large towel, blanket or folded sheet which may serve as a stretcher for two to carry.

If a pill or liquid is to be administered, back the dog in a corner in a sitting position. For a pill, pry back of jaws apart with thumb and forefinger of one hand and with the same fingers of your other hand place pill as far back in dog's throat as possible; close and hold jaws, rubbing throat to cause swallowing. If dog does not gulp, hold one hand over nostrils briefly; he will gulp for air and swallow pill. For liquids, lift the back of the upper lip and tip spoon into the natural pocket formed in the rear of the lower lip; it may be necessary to pull this pocket out with forefinger. Do not give liquids by pouring directly down the dog's throat; this might choke him or make the fluid go down the wrong way.

After treatment keep dog quiet, preferably in his bed or a room where he cannot injure himself or objects.

Bites and Wounds

Clip hair from area. Wash gently with pure soap and water or hydrogen peroxide. If profuse bleeding continues, apply sheet strip or gauze tourniquet between wound and heart but nearest the wound. Release tourniquet briefly at ten-minute intervals. Cold water compresses may stop milder bleeding.

For insect bites and stings, try to remove stinger with tweezers or a dab of cotton, and apply a few drops of ammonia. If dog is in pain, give aspirin at one grain per 10 pounds. (An aspirin tablet is usually 5 grains.)

Burns

Clip hair from area. Apply strong, lukewarm tea (for its tannic acid content) on a sheet strip compress. Vaseline may be used for slight burns. Give aspirin as recommended if dog is in pain. Keep him warm if he seems to be in shock.

Constipation

Give mineral oil: one-quarter teaspoon up to 10 pounds; half teaspoon from 10 to 25 pounds; full teaspoon from 25 to 75 pounds; three-quarters tablespoon over 75 pounds.

Diarrhea

Give kaopectate in same doses by size as indicated for mineral oil above, but repeat within four and eight hours.

Fighting

Do not try forcibly to separate dogs. If available throw a pail of cold water on them. A sharp rap on the rump of each combatant with a strap or stick may help. A heavy towel or blanket dropped over the head of the aggressor, or a newspaper twisted into a torch, lighted and held near them, may discourage the fighters. If a lighted newspaper is used, be careful that sparks do not fall or blow on dogs.

Fits

Try to get the dog into a room where he cannot injure himself. If possible, cover him with a towel or blanket. When the fit ends, give aspirin one grain for every 10 pounds.

Nervousness

Remove cause or remove the dog from the site of the cause. Give the recommended dose of aspirin. Aspirin acts as a tranquilizer.

245

Poisoning

If container of the poison is handy, use recommended antidote printed thereon. Otherwise, make a strong solution of household salt in water and force as much as possible into the dog's throat using the lip pocket method. Minutes count with several poisons; if veterinarian cannot be reached immediately, try to get dog to an MD or registered nurse.

Shock

If dog has chewed electric cord, protect hand with rubber glove or thick dry towel and pull cord from socket. If dog has collapsed, hold ammonia under its nose or apply artificial respiration as follows: place dog on side with its head low, press on abdomen and rib cage, releasing pressure at one- or two-second intervals. Keep dog warm.

Stomach Upsets

For mild stomach disorders, milk of bismuth in same doses as recommended for mineral oil under *Constipation* will be effective. For more severe cases brandy in the same doses but diluted with an equal volume of water may be helpful.

Swallowing Foreign Objects

If object is still in mouth or throat, reach in and remove it. If swallowed, give strong salt solution as for *Poisoning*. Some objects that are small, smooth or soft may not give trouble.

Porcupines and Skunks

Using tweezers or pliers, twist quills one full turn and pull out. Apply hydrogen peroxide to bleeding wounds. For skunk spray, wash dog in tomato juice.

WARNING! Get your dog to a veterinarian *soonest* for severe bites, wounds, burns, poisoning, fits and shock.

27

Skin Troubles

THERE is a tendency on the part of the amateur dog keeper to consider any lesion of the dog's skin to be mange. Mange is an unusual condition in clean, well fed, and well cared for dogs. Eczema occurs much more frequently and is often more difficult to control.

MANGE OR SCABIES

There are at least two kinds of mange that effect dogs—sarcoptic mange and demodectic or red mange, the latter rare indeed and difficult to cure.

Sarcoptic mange is caused by a tiny spider-like mite (*Sarcoptes scabiei canis*) which is similar to the mite that causes human scabies or "itch." Indeed, the mange is almost identical with scabies and is transmissible from dog to man. The mite is approximately 1/100th of an inch in length and without magnification is just visible to acute human sight.

Only the female mites are the cause of the skin irritation. They burrow into the upper layers of the skin, where each lays twenty to forty eggs, which in three to seven days hatch into larvae. These larvae in turn develop into nymphs which later grow into adults. The entire life cycle requires from fourteen to twenty-one days for completion. The larvae, nymphs, and males do not burrow into the skin, but live under crusts and scabs on the surface.

The disease may make its first appearance on any part of the dog's body, although it is usually first seen on the head and muzzle, around the eyes, or at the base of the ears. Sometimes it is first noticed in the armpits, the inner parts of the thighs, the lower abdomen or on the front of the chest. If not promptly treated it may cover the whole body and an extremely bad infestation may cause the death of the dog after a few months.

Red points which soon develop into small blisters are the first signs of the disease. These are most easily seen on the unpigmented parts of the skin, such as the abdomen. As the female mites burrow into the skin, there is an exudation of serum which dries and scabs. The affected parts soon are covered with bran-like scales followed with grayish crusts. The itching is intense, especially in hot weather or after exercise. The rubbing and scratching favor secondary bacterial infections and the formation of sores. The hair may grow matted and fall out, leaving bare spots. The exuded serum decomposes and gives rise to a peculiar mousy odor which increases as the disease develops and which is especially characteristic.

Sarcoptic mange is often confused with demodectic (red) mange, ringworm, or with simple eczema. If there is any doubt about the diagnosis, a microscopic examination of the scrapings of the lesions will reveal the true facts.

It is easy to control sarcoptic mange if it is recognized in its earlier stages and treatment is begun immediately. Neglected, it may be very difficult to eradicate. If it is considered how rapidly the causative mites reproduce themselves, the necessity for early treatment becomes apparent. That treatment consists not only of medication of the dog but also of sterilization of his bedding, all tools and implements used on him, and the whole premises upon which he has been confined. Sarcoptic mange is easily and quickly transmissible from dog to dog, from area to area on the same dog, and even from dog to human.

In some manner which is not entirely understood, an inadequate or unbalanced diet appears to predispose a dog to sarcoptic mange, and few dogs adequately fed and cared for ever contract it. Once a dog has contracted mange, however, improvement in the amount of quality of his food seems not to hasten his recovery.

There are various medications recommended for sarcoptic mange, sulphur ointment being the old standby. However, it is messy, difficult to use, and not always effective. For the treatment of sarcoptic mange, there are available today such insecticides as lindane, chlordane, and DDT. The use of these chemicals greatly facilitates treatment and cure of the dogs affected with mange and those exposed to it.

A bath made by dissolving four ounces of derris powder (containing at least 5% rotenone) and one ounce of soap in one gallon of water has proved effective, especially if large areas of the surface of the dog's skin are involved. All crusts and scabs should be removed before its application. The solution must be well scrubbed into the skin with a moderately stiff brush and the whole animal thoroughly soaked. Only the surplus liquid should be taken off with a towel and the remainder must be permitted to dry on the dog. This bath should be repeated at intervals of five days until all signs of mange have disappeared. Three such baths will usually suffice.

The advantage of such all over treatment is that it protects uninfected areas from infection. It is also a precautionary measure to bathe in this solution uninfected dogs which have been in contact with the infected one.

Isolated mange spots may be treated with oil of lavender. Roll a woolen cloth into a swab with which the oil of lavender can be applied and rubbed in thoroughly for about five minutes. This destroys all mites with which the oil of lavender comes into contact.

Even after a cure is believed to be accomplished, vigilance must be maintained to prevent fresh infestations and to treat new spots immediately if they appear.

DEMODECTIC OR RED MANGE

Demodectic mange, caused by the wormlike mite *Demodex canis,* which lives in the hair follicles and the sebaceous glands of the skin, is difficult to cure. It is a baffling malady of which the prognosis is not favorable. The life cycle of the causative organism is not well understood, the time required from the egg to maturity being so far unknown. The female lays eggs which hatch into young of appearance similar to that of the adult, except that they are smaller and have but three pairs of legs instead of four.

One peculiar feature about demodectic mange is that some dogs appear to be genetically predisposed to it while others do not contract it whatever their contact with infected animals may be. Young animals seem to be especially prone to it, particularly those with short hair. The first evidence of its presence is the falling out of the hair on certain areas of the dog. The spots may be somewhat reddened, and they commonly occur near the eyes, on the hocks, elbows, or toes, although they may be on any part of the dog's body. No itching occurs at the malady's inception, and it never grows so intense as in sarcoptic mange.

In the course of time, the hairless areas enlarge, and the skin attains a copper hue; in severe cases it may appear blue or leadish gray. During this period the mites multiply and small pustules develop. Secondary invasions may occur to complicate the situation. Poisons are formed by the bacteria in the pustules, and the absorption of toxic materials deranges the body functions and eventually affects the whole general health of the dog, leading to emaciation, weakness, and the development of an acrid, unpleasant odor.

This disease is slow and subtle in its development, runs a casual course, and frequently extends over a period of two or even three years. Unless it is treated, it usually terminates in death, although spontaneous recovery occasionally occurs, especially if the dog has been kept on a nourishing diet. As in other skin diseases, correct nutrition plays a major part in recovery from demodectic mange, as it plays an even larger part in its prevention.

It is possible to confuse demodectic mange with sarcoptic mange, fungus infection, acne, or eczema. A definite diagnosis is possible only from microscopic examination of skin scrapings and of material from the pustules. The possibility of demodectic mange, particularly in its earlier stages, is not negated by the failure to find the mites under the microscope, and several examinations may be necessary to arrive at a definite diagnosis.

The prognosis is not entirely favorable. It may appear that the mange is cured and a new and healthy coat may be re-established only to have the disease manifest itself in a new area, and the whole process of treatment must be undertaken afresh.

In the treatment of demodectic mange, the best results have been obtained by the persistent use of benzine hexachloride, chlordane, rotenone, and 2-mercapto benzothiazole. Perseverance is necessary, but even then failure is possible.

EAR MITES OR EAR MANGE

The mites responsible for ear mange (*Ododectes cynotis*) are considerably larger than the ones which cause sarcoptic mange. They inhabit the external auditory canal and are visible to the unaided eye as minute, slowly moving, white objects. Their life history is not known, but is probably similar to that of the mite that causes sarcoptic mange.

These mites do not burrow into the skin, but are found deep in the ear canal, near the eardrum. Considerable irritation results from their presence, and the normal secretions of the ear are interfered with. The ear canal is filled with inflammatory products, modified ear wax, and mites, causing the dog to scratch and rub its ears and to shake its head. While ear mange is not caused by incomplete washing or inefficient drying of the ears, it is encouraged by such negligence.

The ear mange infestation is purely local and is no cause for anxiety. An ointment containing benzine hexachloride is very effective in correcting this condition. The ear should be treated every third or fourth day.

ECZEMA

Eczema is probably the most common of all ailments seen in the dog. Oftentimes it is mistaken for mange or ringworm, although there is no actual relationship between the conditions. Eczema is variously referred to by such names as "hot spots," "fungitch," and "kennel itch."

Some years ago there was near-unanimity of opinion among dog people that the food of the animal was the major contributing factor of eczema. Needless to say, the manufacturers of commercial dog foods were besieged with complaints. Some research on the cause of eczema placed most of the blame on outside environmental factors, and with some help from other sources it was found that a vegetative organism was the causative agent in a great majority of the cases.

Some dogs do show an allergic skin reaction to certain types of protein given to them as food, but this is generally referred to as the "foreign protein" type of dermatitis. It manifests itself by raising numerous welts on the skin, and occasionally the head, face, and ears will become alarmingly swollen. This condition can be controlled by the injection of antihistamine products and subsequent dosage with antihistaminic tablets or capsules such as chlortrimenton or benedryl. Whether "foreign protein" dermatitis is due to an allergy or whether it is due to some toxin manufactured and elaborated by the individual dog is a disputed point.

Most cases of eczema start with reddening of the skin in certain parts. The areas most affected seem to be the region along the spine and at the base of the tail. In house dogs this may have its inception from enlarged and plugged anal glands. The glands when full and not naturally expressed are a source of irritation. The dog will rub his hind parts on the grass in order to alleviate the itching sensation. Fleas, lice, and ticks may be inciting factors, causing the dog to rub and roll in the grass in an attempt to scratch the itchy parts.

In hunting dogs, it is believed that the vegetative cover through which the dogs hunt causes the dermatitis. In this class of dogs the skin becomes irritated and inflamed in the armpits, the inner surfaces of the thighs, and along the belly. Some hunting dogs are bedded down in straw or hay, and such dogs invariably show a general reddening of the skin and a tendency to scratch.

As a general rule, the difference between moist and dry eczema lies in the degree to which the dog scratches the skin with his feet or chews it with his teeth. The inflammation ranges from a simple reddening of the skin to the development of papules, vesicles, and pustules with a discharge. Crusts and scabs like dandruff may form, and if the condition is not treated, it will become chronic and then next to impossible to treat with any success. In such cases the skin becomes thickened and may be pigmented. The hair follicles become infected, and the lesions are constantly inflamed and exuding pus.

When inflammation occurs between the toes and on the pads of the feet, it closely resembles "athletes foot" in the human. Such inflammation generally causes the hair in the region to turn a reddish brown. The ears, when they are affected, emit a peculiar moldy odor and exude a brownish black substance. It is thought that most cases of canker of the ear are due to a primary invasion of the ear canal by a vegetative fungus. If there is a pustular discharge, it is due to the secondary pus-forming bacteria that gain a foothold after the resistance of the parts is lowered by the fungi.

Some breeds of dogs are more susceptible to skin ailments than are others. However, all breeds of dogs are likely to show some degree of dermatitis if they are exposed to causative factors.

Most cases of dermatitis are seen in the summer time, which probably accounts for their being referred to as "summer itch" or "hot spots." The warm moist days of summer seem to promote the growth and development of both fleas and fungi. When the fleas bite the dog, the resulting irritation causes the dog to scratch or bite to alleviate the itch. The area thus becomes moist and makes a perfect place for fungi spores to propagate. That the fungi are the cause of the trouble seems evident, because most cases respond when treated externally with a good fungicide. Moreover, the use of a powder containing both an insecticide and a fungicide tends to prevent skin irritation. Simply dusting the dog once or twice a week with a good powder of the type mentioned is sound procedure in the practice of preventive medicine.

(Editor's note: I have had some success with hydrogen peroxide in treating mild skin troubles. Saturate a cotton pad with a mixture of 2 parts 3% hydrogen peroxide to 1 part boiled water. Apply, but do NOT rub, to affected skin. Let dry naturally and when *completely* dry apply an antiseptic talcum powder like Johnson & Johnson's Medicated Powder. When this treatment was suggested to my veterinarian, he confirmed that he had had success with it. If the skin irritation is not noticeably better after two of these treatments, once daily, the case should be referred to a veterinarian.)

RINGWORM

Ringworm is a communicable disease of the skin of dogs, readily transmissible to man and to other dogs and animals. The disease is caused by specific fungi, which are somewhat similar to ordinary molds. The lesions caused by ringworm usually first appear on the face, head, or legs of the dog, but they may occur on any part of the surface of his body.

The disease in dogs is characterized by small, circular areas of dirty gray or brownish-yellow crusts or scabs partially devoid of hair, the size of a dime. As the disease progresses, the lesions increase both in size and in number and merge to form larger patches covered with crusts containing broken off hair. A raw, bleeding surface may appear when crusts are broken or removed by scratching or rubbing to relieve itching. In some cases, however, little or no itching is manifested. Microscopic examination and culture tests are necessary for accurate diagnosis.

If treatment of affected dogs is started early, the progress of the disease can be immediately arrested. Treatment consists of clipping the hair from around the infected spots, removing the scabs and painting the spots with tincture of iodine, five percent salicylic acid solution, or other fungicide two or three times weekly until recovery takes place. In applying these remedies it is well to cover the periphery of the circular lesion as well as its center, since the spots tend to expand outward from their centers. Scabs, hair, and debris removed from the dog during his treatments should be burned to destroy the causative organisms and to prevent reinfection. Precautions in the handling of animals affected with ringworm should be observed to preclude transmission to man and other animals. Isolation of affected dogs is not necessary if the treatment is thorough.

Ch. Leif of Dragondell, C.D.X., T.D. at age of six years, with his 3-month-old daughter, Leiflet.

A remarkable photograph of the Norwegian Elkhound as an Obedience performer. Ch. Leif of Dragondell, C.D.X., T.D., pictured taking jump while training for his C.D.X. degree. Leif was owned by the Hon. William H. Timbers.